# SAGAS OF THE Central Coast

History from the Pages of
**Central Coast**
The Magazine
of Pleasures and Pursuits

Bob Nelson, Publisher

# TABLE OF CONTENTS

# THE WRITERS

SINCE ITS INAUGURAL issue in 1983, *Central Coast* magazine has relied on local free-lance writers for much of its editorial content. Working closely with the publisher and utilizing their own research and writing skills, these writers are responsible for the magazine's reputation for producing lively, accurate stories on Central Coast history. Their efforts have been instrumental in making this book possible:

*Central Coast* magazine publisher **Bob Nelson** established the publication's emphasis on local history while writing many of the stories. He draws on 20 years of experience in publishing. After moving to the Central Coast from Illinois in 1979, he now resides in Orcutt.

**Melissa Abramovitz** of San Luis Obispo juggles family life with a writing career that has seen her nonfiction articles, short stories and poems published in magazines for children, teenagers and adults. Her award-winning first novel, *Dependent Variables*, was published in 1992.

**Jon C. Picciuolo** has become an expert on the history of the Lompoc Valley and its surroundings. Retired from naval intelligence, he lives in Vandenberg Village where he is an elected director of the community services district. He also writes short stories, many of which have been published in small magazines across the country.

A fifth-generation native of the Central Coast, **January Anderson** has produced hundreds of articles about the area for a variety of local publications. Living and writing in Glendale since 1990, she remains a popular contributor to *Central Coast* magazine.

War correspondent, newspaper editor, author of 17 books, **Phillip H. Ault** also shared his knowledge of history with *Central Coast* magazine readers. Today residing in Sun City, AZ, he is completing the fourth edition of his popular educational work, *Public Relations Strategies and Tactics.*

A retired teacher who also contributed to Cleveland newspapers for three decades, **Marilyn Schobel** moved to Orcutt in 1990.

Community liaison officer at Vandenberg Air Force Base, Lt. Col **Cary Gray** has been writing about the Central Coast since moving here in 1986.

I N CHICAGO, where I grew up, history is part of life. Even schoolchildren who cringe at the thought of opening a U.S. History book know something about the city's past. Much of it is colorful—The Great Chicago Fire, baseball's Black Sox scandal, Al Capone and his gangsters, etc.—and Chicagoans have a wry sense of pride in their history, celebrating it in literature, song and throughout the city's culture.

While growing up, my interest in Chicago's history was quickly eclipsed by affection for the Old West. In the 1950s the media had a love affair with the western. There were gold mines, wagon trains, sprawling ranches, breathtaking vistas, and heroes espousing simple truths. Sure, this version of history was romanticized and sanitized, but it served a greater purpose by lionizing the colorful, can-do people who populated the region during a fabulous era.

Imbued with an appreciation for Old West history, I brought my family to the Central Coast in 1979, and I was surprised and slightly disappointed to see how little attention locals apparently paid to their past. I found a restored mission here and a fine historical museum there, but I expected every community to be immersed in its history. Families handed down wonderful stories from generation to generation, but otherwise history seemed to be locked away in a cultural closet. When *Central Coast* magazine began publishing in 1983, we decided to clean out the closet.

With the assistance of other devotees of Central Coast history, we discovered scores of thrilling, dramatic and funny stories that we felt matched those of any other area of the West. Readers responded enthusiastically, and why not? For these stories were not filled with the obscure dates and names and rather meaningless events that bogged down the history books of school days. No, these stories were about real people, with flaws and strengths and fears, who were caught up in the swirl of events of nation-building.

Through the years, readers regularly told us how much they enjoyed a particular article from a past issue and asked whether we could gather a bunch of them into a book. Hence, *Sagas of the Central Coast.*

We collected 36 of our most-requested stories, placing them into three sections: Pioneer Days, Growing Up and Modern Times. While presenting a compelling cast of characters and events, *Sagas of the Central Coast* also provides a story-by-story time line of the development of the region.

Preparing this publication allowed me to lose myself in the history of the Central Coast and rekindle a youthful enthusiasm for our heritage. Perhaps it will do the same for you.

Enjoy.

BOB NELSON, EDITOR AND PUBLISHER
October 1994

# FOREWORD

# ACKNOWLEDGEMENTS

THIS BOOK project was encouraged and assisted by others in the community with an equal affection for our history. They include Marilyn Cronk and the board of directors of the Santa Maria Valley Historical Society; Myra Manfrina and the Lompoc Valley Historical Society; and Gordon Bennett of the Bennett-Loomis archives. Also helping were Lesley Benn of the Gerber Collection, the Orcutt Historical Committee and Norm Hammond.

The production team consisted of Dr. Joe Ziemba, our longtime copy editor; Mila Good of Good Graphics and Design, who designed the interior pages; and Amy Color and Chris Dillman of Amy Color Creative Concepts, who designed the cover.

Through the years many other people supported our efforts, including Winston Wickenden, Jim Norris, Jennifer L. Stockdale, Marian Hancock, Floyd Antonides and Larry Viegas.

We are in their debt.

# SECTION I

## PIONEER DAYS
## 1824-1899

# INDIAN REVOLT
## AT
## LA PURISIMA

THE BEAUTIFULLY restored La Purisima Mission, now a California state park near Lompoc, was not always as peaceful as it appears today.

In early 1824, the California missions were mired in hard times. More than a decade of revolt in Mexico had eliminated the primary source of territorial operating funds. The Mexican military government of California now demanded that the missions pay heavily for the soldiers garrisoned in them. Adding to the missions' miserable predicament were a sharply declining Indian population and the ever-increasing arrogance of the soldiers.

The young Chumash Indians of the Central Coast missions of La Purisima, Santa Inez and Santa Barbara bitterly resented the endless demands to feed, clothe and equip the idle soldiers. They were weary of subjugation and were undoubtedly inspired by the stirring tales of civil insurrection coming out of Mexico.

Mission priests and some of the older Indians counseled patience, vainly trying to kindle hope for better times. But by mid-February, Indian tempers rose precipitously, and bows and arrows were stockpiled. Only a small spark was needed to set off the powder keg.

On the morning of Saturday, February 21, the Indians of Santa Inez Mission became enraged by the flogging of a young La Purisima Chumash convert at the hands of a Santa Inez corporal. They attacked the Santa Inez military garrison with arrows and set fire to the mission buildings before being beaten down by a force of soldiers from Santa Barbara. Indian riders spread the word of the revolt to La Purisima and Santa Barbara, igniting insurrection at those missions.

At La Purisima, the fighting was particularly violent. By 3 p.m. February 21 a pitched battle was raging. Cpl. Tiburcio Tapia, the senior soldier of the garrison, had managed to gather his four men, their wives and families, and the mission's two priests into a burnt-out shell of a building. The Indians attacked them and set fire to the other structures of the mission. Tapia and his men answered the Indian arrows with musket fire, killing seven Chumash and suffering no losses. A soldier's wife was slightly wounded by an arrow.

That evening, after much Chumash bloodshed, an Indian spokesman offered a truce. The soldiers would be allowed to evacuate to Santa Inez, he said, only if they lay down their arms. Cpl. Tapia, unwilling to trust the Indian, scorned the offer, saying that he and his men would rather die at their posts. That night, four hapless travelers on their way to Los Angeles accidentally stumbled into the fray and were slain by the Indians.

The stalemate was broken by the intercession of the Rev. Blas Ordaz, the junior of the two La Purisima priests. He argued in favor of the Indian proposal and encouraged the soldiers to take the Chumash at their word. Finally, Cpl. Tapia and his men reluctantly laid down their arms. There was a tense moment when it appeared that some of the young

Indians were preparing to slaughter the unarmed soldiers; but the Rev. Ordaz and the Chumash leader quickly restored the truce.

The evacuation was particularly hard for the wives and children of the garrison. They had to walk 15 miles to the relative safety of the burnt-out Santa Inez mission. The soldiers left behind all their hand weapons and two rusty old *pedreros* (small swivel cannons) which had mostly been used by the mission to fire noisy salutes on feast days.

Only one non-Indian, the Rev. Antonio Rodriguez, remained at La Purisima. The Indians apparently had no quarrel with the missionary priest and tolerated his presence.

The rebellious Indians now realized that harsh retaliation would be certain and soon. Reinforced by other rebels streaming in from Santa Inez, they began to fortify the mission for the expected assault. The two swivel cannons were mounted, log barricades were erected, and firing-holes were cut through the charred adobe walls of the church and other buildings. However, perhaps because of a powder shortage, there was little marksmanship practice; this proved critical in the battle to come.

Meanwhile, news of the revolt reached Gov. Luis Arguello in Monterey. He reacted as swiftly as possible. A small army consisting of infantry, cavalry, and artillerymen, and including one cannon, was dispatched on March 14 from San Luis Obispo under the command of Lt. Jose Maria Estrada. By the dark, early morning hours of March 16, after a forced march over the coastal hills, the tiny army of 109 men was poised for an assault on La Purisima.

Lt. Estrada positioned his cavalry to the right and left of the mission buildings to cut off any escape by the Indians. Then he wheeled his cannon forward until it was within range of the mission. At 8 a.m., the four-pounder opened fire, blowing a great hole in the Indian defenses. At the same time, his men poured well-aimed musket fire into the adobe walls.

The Chumash replied with arrows and musket fire. There was also an attempt by the Indians to return fire using their little swivel cannons; but one of these old weapons exploded,

**La Purisima Mission prior to its 20th-century restoration.**

*Photo/Lompoc Valley Historical Society*

3

causing heavy loss of life. The marksmanship and tactics of the Indians were no match for those of Estrada's men. By 10:30 a.m. the battle was over; Rev. Rodriguez arranged for a cease fire, bravely walking out of the mission to talk truce.

Three of Estrada's men were wounded, one fatally. Sixteen Chumash lay dead and many more were wounded. When the smoke cleared, Lt. Estrada's men took possession of 16 muskets, 150 lances, six cutlasses, what was left of the swivel cannons, and a great number of bows and arrows.

Troops from Santa Barbara, under the command of Capt. de la Guerra, arrived after the Indians had surrendered. Following orders from the governor, Estrada and de la Guerra took depositions from the Indians and, on March 23, passed sentence. On March 26 seven Chumash were executed by firing squad for the murders of the four travelers at the start of the revolt. The four ringleaders of the insurrection were sentenced to 10 years imprisonment in the Presidio of Santa Barbara, followed by perpetual exile from the province. Eight others were sent to the presidio for eight years.

Gov. Arguello thought that his officers had been too lenient in the punishments. Nevertheless, he rewarded his men. Lt. Estrada was promoted one rank and his men were awarded double pay for a month. However, in keeping with the hard times in California which had contributed to the original cause of the revolt, the soldiers never received even their original pay, not to mention the double allowance.

Some historians believe that the failure of the bloody Chumash revolt at La Purisima may have directly prevented a general Indian uprising at all the California missions. But this will never be known for sure.

*By Jon C. Picciuolo, August 1990*

**F**ROM THE FREEWAY, the Price Anniversary House does not look like much more than a large abandoned shack. One can see it from Highway 101 with a glance down Price Canyon, where the railroad tracks take a shortcut behind Pismo Heights toward San Luis Obispo. The 2-story structure, once a charming Victorianesque home, is now paintless and as brown as ploughed soil. Sheets of plywood cover the windows like big blonde stamps.

But to history buffs and the City of Pismo Beach, the house and rural land surrounding it are but an unpolished gem, the potential pride and joy of the seaside city. It is also the means for a tribute to its builder, John Michael Price, an important Central Coast pioneer.

"There are people who live in Pismo Beach who don't even know who Price was," said Susan Desmond, commissioner of the city's Parks and Recreation Department. "They don't realize that he was an important judge. He established the first business licenses in the county, brought the first official school to the county and hired the first school teacher."

Price built his house in the early 1890s as a gift to his wife, Maria Andrea, on the occasion of their 50th wedding anniversary. It was built on part of Price's 7000-acre Pismo Rancho which he had owned since the late 1840s.

When the city acquired the house and four surrounding acres about 10 years ago, plans were formed to restore the house to its original state and develop a park complete with picnic gardens, an information center and a museum.

Raising interest and funding for the project, however, has been a slow process. Desmond said that gathering information for grant applications is long, tedious work—plus it took many years for the local historical society to convince the city that the house was worth restoring. The city eventually declared it a historical site, but during the interim the house had deteriorated.

"There had been transients living in it who had stripped it and destroyed it," Desmond said. "It's in pretty poor shape, but not so bad that we can't restore it. We have been stabilizing the house—weatherproofing it, boarding up the holes, putting a new roof on it, and making it sound so that it can't deteriorate any further. We'll start restoration in the spring."

The house, museum, and gardens are only part of the project's charm, however. According to Jean Hubbard, past president of the South County Historical Society, the compelling personality and adventurous life of John Michael Price alone could merit a museum.

"He was quite a man," she said. "He was only 5-2 and didn't dress like everyone else. He wore a gray-lined duster (a long overcoat), a gray top hat, rode gray horses, and had a little white dog that was always with him—it was sort of like his signature. He had an elegant gray buggy with matched gray horses. He cut quite a figure."

Born in Bristol, England in 1810, he became a sailor on a whaling ship at 15. Cruel treatment on board caused him to jump ship in Mexico; he made his way up to Salinas where he

# THE LIFE AND TIMES OF JOHN MICHAEL PRICE

found work herding cattle on the big ranchos. He eventually came to Nipomo where he served as a vaquero for Capt. W.G. Dana and then worked for landowner Isaac Sparks, who paid Price by giving him the Pismo Rancho and a herd of cattle.

"Sparks joked at the time that he never employed a man who was smarter than he was, and that was why he was getting rid of Price," Hubbard said.

Being a "foreigner" (not a Mexican citizen) in California during the mid-19th century was risky. In 1840, while working on Dana's Nipomo Rancho, Price was arrested by a party of soldiers under the direction of Gov. Alvarado and charged with being a revolutionist. Along with 160 other Americans, he was taken to Monterey and thrown into an adobe dungeon with a single small hole for air and mud floor (it was during the rainy season). There was no bedding or chairs and very little food and water.

The prisoners were taken to Mexico for trial. After six months, Price and the others were set free, since conspiracy could not be proven. Most of the prisoners settled for a compensation payment of $400, but Price and 14 others held out, demanding to be returned home to California and paid in full for their losses. He won.

Price was heavily involved in the politics of the day. Under Mexican rule he served as "alcalde" and was the sole determiner of law and order from San Miguel to Nipomo. He maintained the position during the transition from Mexican to American rule in 1850, becoming judge, sheriff and county supervisor. At that time, San Luis Obispo County was plagued by bandits.

*'He put together the City of Pismo Beach in the 1880s'*

"In one instance, he came home from a trip and found that his family had just been robbed," Hubbard said. "He had a pretty good idea that the robbers had gone up in the canyon to the family picnic grounds. Sure enough, he was right. He had a shoot-out with them, got his money, and went home. His wife was quite upset because he'd been shot in the leg. She pulled his boot off and it was full of blood."

Price's Pismo Rancho covered the area from present-day Pirate's Cove south of Avila Beach to the old Catholic cemetery about a mile north of Oak Park Road near Arroyo Grande. In 1882 he built a wharf and hotel at Pismo Beach to facilitate shipping of grain to market.

"He put together the City of Pismo Beach in the 1880s," Hubbard said. "It was Price who laid it out and sold large sections of it to developers like Dolliver and Pomeroy (Pismo's main streets are named after them). Normally it was little buildings and hotels, but in the summertime it was a big tent city. There were dozens of wooden platforms covered by blue and white striped tents which were rented to people for vacationing."

Price remained a respected member of the community until he died at age 92 in 1902. In the years since, Price's original rancho has been broken up into smaller parcels, although much of the Price Canyon property is still used for

In the dangerous early days of the
Central Coast, John Michael Price was
rarely seen without a canine friend—
and his weapon.

cattle ranching and farming. The rural setting of the Anniversary House, in fact, makes it rare among historical California homes, Desmond said. "I think there is only one other such house in the state that has that much land around it—that isn't right downtown," she said.

Desmond said the house, once restored, will remain faithful to its era. There will be no electricity or bathrooms, even though one was added in 1902 for an aging Mrs. Price, who could no longer make the trip to the outhouses in the back.

"It won't be the 'Frilly Priscilla' kind of house, because that's not the way they lived," she said. "It was very simple, really."

Even though the house is empty and dilapidated, Desmond said it has a rich aura. "You can feel what was going on there," she declared. "It's like it's sitting there, just waiting to be dressed up and looked at."

*By January Anderson, March 1988*

**Note: At this printing, restoration of the Price Anniversary House is continuing, slowly but surely.**

A TREMOR OF ANXIETY spread through calm, pastoral, isolated Central California in December 1846.

Vaqueros raced between settlements and ranchos like Mexican Paul Reveres, alerting the populace with an ominous warning: the Americans are coming.

Mexico and the United States were at war and the Mexican province of Alta California—with little communication to the capital in Mexico City and defended by only a few hundred troops—was ripe for conquest.

The land-hungry Americans, pushing to the Pacific behind their banner of Manifest Destiny, claimed California for themselves after capturing the provincial capital of Monterey early in 1846. But the rest of the huge region remained to be subjugated.

Meanwhile, British warships waited off the coast for an opportunity to grab a chunk of the province if the Americans faltered. Russians operating from Alaska had already established Fort Ross north of San Francisco and appeared poised to overrun the territory.

The Americans moved aggressively to consolidate their gains. Lt. Col. John C. Fremont left Monterey in late Novem-

# Foxen and Fremont: A Christmas Story

**British expatriate Benjamin Foxen, a Mexican citizen by marriage, threw in his lot with John Fremont and his invading American army.**
*Photo/Santa Maria Valley Historical Society*

ber with orders to link up near present-day Los Angeles with a force commanded by Commodore Robert Stockton, fighting its way north from San Diego.

Fremont—with a reputation as an explorer that would one day give him the title "The Great Pathfinder"—rode at the head of a 430-man force labeled the "California Battalion." It was a wild and scruffy army of sailors and mountain men, blacks and Indians, professional soldiers and recent immigrants. All were adventurers.

Although few shots were fired during the California Battalion's march down the Central Coast, fear accompanied news of its approach. Fear turned to panic after the force occupied San Luis Obispo. Fremont planned to execute a captured Californian but relented only after a tearful plea from the condemned man's wife.

The Americans found only deserted homes as they traveled toward the Santa Maria Valley. Supplies were a problem and drought left little good grass for the expedition's hundreds of horses and mules.

The famished, rag-tag army arrived December 21 at Rancho Tinaquaic, owned by British expatriate Benjamin Foxen. The Americans helped themselves to Foxen's cattle. The rancher, who had not heeded the vaqueros' call to leave, welcomed Fremont to his domain.

Foxen faced a momentous decision.

California had been good to him since he arrived as a sailor and settled near Santa Barbara in 1817. He married Eduarda Osuna, daughter of a local official, accepted the Catholic faith and became a Mexican citizen. He later obtained the 8800-acre Rancho Tinaquaic and built an imposing adobe ranch house for his family at the head of what is now Foxen Canyon.

But Foxen sensed the weakness of the Mexican regime and the corresponding strength of the American republic. He made the agonizing decision to throw in his lot with Fremont and the Americans.

Through his wife, Foxen heard rumors that the Californians in Santa Barbara were preparing to ambush Fremont's force at Gaviota Pass.

Fremont's scouts had come to a similar conclusion. Gaviota Pass—"the Pass of the Gulls"—at that time was a narrow defile between walls of granite. A wagon could barely pass; men would have to march two abreast.

The scouts reported that the pass, closely watched by Californian scouts, was an ideal place for the enemy to roll boulders down on Fremont's men as they worked their way through the gorge.

Fremont spoke to Foxen, who offered himself and his eldest son, William, as guides for another route across San Marcos Pass, once used by Indians and explorers but forgotten for decades.

The California Battalion, led by the Foxens, left Rancho Tinaquaic and marched toward Santa Ynez. Near that town's

*Foxen sensed the weakness of the Mexican regime and the corresponding strength of the American republic*

mission the force detoured from the road toward Gaviota Pass and into the Santa Ynez Mountains.

On a dreary, rainy Christmas Eve they worked their way along the narrows and canyons and spent Christmas night at the top of the ridge.

In *Fremont, Explorer for a Restless Nation*, author Ferol Egan described the scene:

"Though the view from the camp on the ridge was splendid, and the men could see the towers of the mission (Santa Barbara) and the great expanse of the Pacific, they also saw a steep slope that would be tough going for men and animals.

"Christmas 1846 came as no gift. It wasn't until noon that the men dragging the heavy cannons made it to the top of the ridge. By then the rain was falling so hard it was nearly impossible to see, and the wind whipped in from the Pacific with almost the force of a tornado."

All that day and far into the night the army inched down the mountain. Horses and mules fell to their deaths or drowned in rain-swollen ravines.

The exhausted men arrived at the base of the mountain by twos and threes and slept in mud and water. Although the next day dawned clear and warm, the California Battalion spent most of it salvaging its supplies and animals.

Fremont paid a stiff price to avoid Gaviota Pass. His

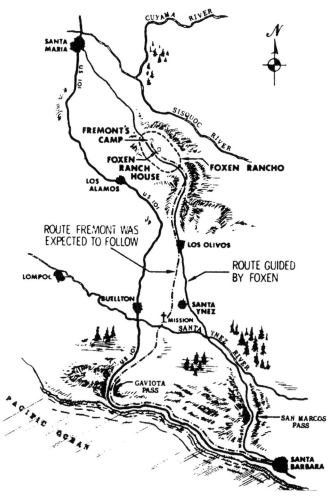

Map shows Fremont's detour to San Marcos Pass.

battered force was minus dozens of mounts as it marched without incident into Santa Barbara on the afternoon of December 27. As a note of irony, he learned that the Californians had deserted Gaviota Pass long before his expected arrival and most had fled Santa Barbara toward the south.

After this bloodless victory the pace of conquest quickened. With only slight interference from the Californians, Fremont marched to his rendezvous with Stockton. Resistance collapsed, and on January 13, 1847—19 days after Fremont descended from San Marcos Pass—Mexico ceded California to the United States.

And what of Foxen? His shift in allegiance cost him dearly.

The Californians considered him a traitor. His adobe home was burned three times, his grazing lands were plundered, his life threatened.

He abandoned Rancho Tinaquaic, eventually reaching Santa Barbara. After years as a refugee he returned to his land, now safe under American rule, and later directed the opening of a stagecoach route through San Marcos Pass.

Foxen's descendants still own sections of the rancho. The pioneer's remains lie at the foot of a broken mast in the graveyard of Chapel San Ramon on Foxen Canyon Road.

Santa Marians honored Foxen in 1926 with a monument on the site where Fremont's California Battalion bivouacked before its historic ascent to San Marcos Pass.

At the top of the monument Foxen's name gets equal billing with Fremont's, a tribute to his little-known, yet important role in California history.

*By Bob Nelson, December 1985*

T HE EMINENT CALIFORNIA historian Robert Cleland wrote of Nancy Kelsey that "surely she deserves an enduring place in the heroic records of the state."

Since Kelsey was the first pioneer woman to cross the plains and desert from the United States and enter California from the east by climbing across the trackless crest of the Sierras, Cleland's comment may be an understatement.

Her adventure occurred in 1841, eight years before the Gold Rush when Mexico still owned the region. She was 18 years old, barefoot and hungry, and carried her infant daughter in her arms.

This is the stuff of history, indeed. But fate deals its hands unpredictably. Almost forgotten, today Kelsey lies in a solitary grave deep in the mountains east of Santa Maria alongside the creek in Cottonwood Canyon.

It is a remote and humble resting place for a dauntless woman with a remarkable story. During a half century of wandering, she survived Indian fights and participated in the Bear Flag revolt. Terrified, she saw one of her daughters scalped by Indians. She knew Kit Carson, baked bread for John C. Fremont, grew temporarily rich from the Gold Rush,

# ADVENTURES
# OF A
# FRONTIER
# HEROINE

**Nancy Kelsey was the first pioneer woman to cross the western desert and climb the Sierra into California.**

*Photo/Santa Maria Valley Historical Society*

fled through the woods from bears, and along the way bore 10 children.

Kelsey died at 73, an impoverished widow, in a flimsy cabin a short distance from the gravesite—a cabin described by a young woman who helped her during a vain fight against cancer as "almost as remote from civilization in those days as if it were a lonely island in the sea."

In the final years of her often perilous life, Kelsey's contact with the outer world was through sympathetic friends in Santa Maria.

They came to know her because occasionally she made the two-day trip by wagon along the 50-mile Cuyama River-Tepusquet Canyon route to the little farm town of 1500 people. She brought chickens grown on her small patch of canyon land to sell in town.

Nancy Roberts married Ben Kelsey, 10 years her senior, in Missouri in 1838 when she was 15. A year later she had a daughter, Martha Ann, and then a son who died shortly after birth. Only a few weeks after this grief, the Kelseys joined a wagon train that creaked westward out of Missouri in May 1841.

At Soda Springs, in present-day Idaho, the emigrant train split. One group continued northwest to Oregon, the other turned southwest toward California. Known to historians as the Bartleson-Bidwell party, the latter consisted of 30 men, Nancy, and baby Martha Ann.

Soon their sufferings became intense.

Without a map, they became lost. They had to abandon their wagons and push ahead with oxen and horses. When food ran short, they ate the oxen, then a horse. Exhausted and half-starved, they finally crossed the top of the Sierra in October near what is now known as Sonora Pass.

On the westward descent into California, four pack animals fell over a bluff, carrying with them all the remaining supplies. For two days, the pioneers survived on acorns. Eventually the Kelseys reached Sutter's Fort near present-day Sacramento on Christmas Day, after seven months on the trail.

After that ordeal, one might have expected these pioneers to settle down. Most members of the Bartleson-Bidwell party did, but Nancy Kelsey discovered that she had married a wanderer. Her husband had restless feet and the instincts of a wheeler-dealer. For the rest of their lives, they kept moving in pursuit of his schemes.

These were rough people, crude-tongued and skimpily educated, more at home in a hunting camp than in a proper Victorian parlor. Kelsey said she supposed that she could remember her youth so well "because my mind is not stuffed so full of education as most minds are at this age."

With his earnings as a hunter for Sutter's Fort, Ben bought 100 cattle. He and Nancy, in company with another party, set out to drive the cattle 600 miles north to the Columbia River for sale to Oregon settlers.

*These were rough people, crude-tongued and skimpily educated, more at home in a hunting camp than in a proper Victorian parlor*

As the men struggled to get the cattle across the upper Sacramento River, nude Indians with bows and arrows raided the camp where Nancy waited. The white men's guns prevailed in the fight that followed. As a rifleman watched, gun ready, one Indian was forced to swim across the river, towing to safety a canoe in which Nancy and her daughter rode.

During the next few years, the Kelseys turned up in many places—a cattle drive to what is now Eureka on the northern coast, a trading post on the Sacramento River, a flour mill near Sonoma, a toll ferry Ben built on the Kern River, and a log cabin in the Napa Valley.

As the talk of rebellion against Mexican rule stirred, Ben went to Sonoma and Nancy followed from Napa.

Later she recalled, "I was sent to Fort Sonoma and rode the distance on horseback and carried a 1-month-old babe in my arms. I was so weak when I arrived at my destination that I could not stand up."

Nancy was one of several women who sewed the original Bear Flag for the uprising, using scraps of material. California's state flag evolved from that crude device.

At news that gold had been discovered, Ben headed for the diggings. Returning proudly to their cabin with his saddlebags full of gold, he told Nancy, "If you can lift the bags, you can have it all." She couldn't, of course.

Ever restless, in about 1860 the Kelseys began a 1000-mile trek to Arizona, Mexico and Texas that proved to be disastrous.

In 1861 they were in west Texas with some other wanderers. Ben and the men had left their camp to hunt wild turkeys when a band of Comanches appeared. The two older Kelsey girls ran to hide in the brush. Nancy and the other women hid with the small children in a cave at the side of a ravine, from which they heard the Indians overhead hunting them.

Late in life Nancy described the horror that followed. "I had forgotten to hide the money which we had brought along to buy cattle for the California Market." It was $10,000, all the money the Kelseys had in the world.

The Indians pillaged the camp, took the money and started away when they found one of the girls.

"Poor girl. She was only 13 years old, and even now I can hear the screams as they caught her."

The Kelseys found their daughter in the brush the next morning. "My anguish was horrible when I discovered she had been scalped." The girl had suffered 17 cuts from lances but remarkably survived and lived another five years, devastated by the experience.

Back in California, broke, the Kelseys were in Lone Pine at the time of the huge Owens Valley earthquake of 1872. In 1875 they turned up in Lompoc, where the editor of the new *Lompoc Record* in vain urged the development company to give them land for a home. Soon they moved to Los Angeles, where Ben died in 1889.

As a widow, Nancy decided to abandon city living and return to nature. Precisely why she chose Cottonwood Can-

*Ever restless, in about 1860 the Kelseys began a 1000-mile trek to Arizona, Mexico and Texas that proved to be disastrous*

yon is unclear, but probably it was because Martha Ann, the baby she carried across the Sierra, had married a man in Cuyama, some dozen miles to the east. A check of Santa Barbara County files shows that Nancy never officially filed a homestead claim.

Two Santa Marians who became especially interested in her situation were Ida Blochman, educator and civic leader, and Addison Powell, who was responsible for getting Nancy to dictate her fragmentary reminiscences. When Nancy needed milk, Eugene Johnston's father had the young man lead a cow all the way to Cottonwood Canyon for her.

Nancy began to "feel poorly," so Blochman arranged for her to be examined in Santa Maria by Drs. William T. Lucas and H.B. Bagby. They found an inoperable cancer, and she returned to her chicken farm to die.

The pioneer woman's desire was to be buried in a real store coffin, not something knocked together with boards. Money was scarce in the canyons, but the few residents scraped some together. One drove a wagon to Santa Maria, where Nancy's friends collected the remaining funds. The coffin was stored in a cabin near Nancy's until it was needed.

This was a poignant end to a life of endurance, kindliness and loyalty—a life that few today would want to emulate but all can admire.

*By Phillip H. Ault, July 1989*

THE MISSION grounds at San Miguel were ominously quiet that day in October 1848 when John Price and F.Z. Branch, early settlers of the Arroyo Grande Valley, passed on a trip home from the mines on the Stanislaus River.

The two men were good friends of the Read family, who at that time were in possession of Mission San Miguel. Wondering at the fact that none of the Reads came out to greet them, Price and Branch dismounted from their horses and entered the mission building where the Reads made their home.

The carnage they found inside was shocking. There was a body of an infant, whose head had been dashed against a pillar. Further search revealed the bodies of Read, his wife, daughter, son-in-law, two other children and a servant, all brutally murdered.

Price and Branch hurried to Paso Robles and gave the alarm. A party returned to the mission and examined the evidence, and in short order a group of men from throughout San Luis Obispo County, headed by Price and Branch, set out in pursuit of the murderers.

In time, it was learned that the day before Read had been visited by a party of sailors who had deserted a ship-of-war at Monterey. A gregarious man, Read had offered them hospitality, told them of his recent adventures hunting for gold in the Sierra Nevada, showing them several thousand dollars worth of gold dust he had collected.

For a man living unguarded in the wilderness of San Miguel, it was a tragically unwise thing to do.

The sailors had also been unwise; Branch, Price, and their party pursued the murderers relentlessly, chasing them south for days through San Luis Obispo and Santa Barbara counties and on to the coast of Carpinteria, where one of the party was killed and others wounded in a wild gun battle. But in that fight at the Carpinteria seashore, all the murderers were slain, and, according to Thompson and West's 1883 *History of San Luis Obispo County*, their bodies were "left where they fell, as food for the vultures and coyotes."

The incident of San Miguel, while regarded as the first major criminal tragedy in the county, would not be the last, nor would it be the last time that Price, Branch and other community leaders would find themselves taking the law into their own hands.

It was a time of change in California, which had been taken from Mexico by the United States in 1848, becoming a state in 1850. Naturally enough, antagonism between Americans and Mexicans and native Californians, or "Californios," was strong. Since the bulk of the legal citizenry of California was made up of natives, they also made up the juries, and were usually hesitant to convict a fellow countryman of a crime perpetrated against the invading Americans and foreigners.

Too, "banditos" had frightened many otherwise honest native landholders into offering them harbor against Ameri-

# Vigilante Justice

cans, and there were also a few American criminals with political power who were able to convince even the most respectable natives that they could prevent political persecution by protecting them.

Hence, according to *History of San Luis Obispo County*, the criminals "in a measure, rendered trials abortive," and violent crime on the Central Coast became widespread. This made it necessary to organize an extra-judicial power, and in 1858, 150 men from Paso Robles to the Nipomo Mesa (Price and Branch among them) banded together to form the San Luis Obispo Vigilance Committee.

The committee was pioneered by Walter Murray, a lawyer, writer, and printer who settled in San Luis Obispo County in 1853. It is his writings, sent in letters that were published in the *San Francisco Bulletin* and later reprinted in *History of San Luis Obispo County*, that comprise what is known about county vigilantes.

Murray wrote that, in the days following his arrival, "scarcely a month has passed without the disappearance of some traveler, or the finding of dead bodies or skeletons on the roads leading north and south from here."

In his letter, Murray wrote of a peddler who was murdered near San Juan, and how shortly afterward "eight or ten men passed through here ... and, after flourishing around town for a few days, boasting of their misdeeds," left for Los Angeles. A group of citizens chased them down and found them in possession of stolen property of the murdered peddler, whereupon they tried to take the men, killing one in the process. They managed to capture four men, whom they hauled back to San Luis Obispo and promptly hanged.

The courts of the day were not so swift in dealing justice. In November 1857 two Frenchmen bought some cattle at Paso Robles and headed north. A man named Nieves Robles asked if he might join them in their travels to San Jose, and that night, suggested that the group camp on "the dark and bloody ground" near the mouth of the Nacimiento River.

The next morning, the two Frenchmen discovered that some horses were missing from their camp, and, riding in opposite directions from the camp, went in search of them. They never returned.

Several weeks later, the body of one Frenchman was found, his head riddled with bullet holes. An Indian who claimed to have witnessed the murder from afar said the deed had been done by two men on horseback with pistols and riatas.

Nieves Robles was a known companion of the infamous Jack Powers, who, the day before the Frenchmen's disappearance, had learned of their plans to drive the cattle to San Jose while he was at a horse race in Santa Margarita. In his letters, Murray implies that Robles was sent as a spy to the Frenchmen's camp. He also charges that "late discoveries" showed that Powers, Pio Linares, "Huero" (Light Skinned) Rafael, and some others murdered the Frenchmen. Indeed, Murray writes, "So daring and impudent had long impunity

*'Scarcely a month has passed without the disappearance of some traveler, or the finding of dead bodies or skeletons on the roads leading north and south from here'*

made these men that the (planned) murder was almost openly talked of between the bad characters at the horse race the day before."

Shortly after the body was found, Robles "was taken from the gambling table in San Luis" and put in jail; Linares caught wind of it and told Powers, who was then in San Francisco. Powers returned to town forthwith, coffee, liquor, "and other comforts" in hand, and visited Robles in the jailhouse as well as Robles' attorney, whom he urged to have Robles released.

When Robles went to trial, writes Murray, the jury was packed with Californios, among them a fugitive from the charge of murder and another "an accomplice in the very crime for which Robles was tried." Robles was set free, and law-abiding Americans and foreigners were outraged yet helpless.

Scarcely seven months later, two French settlers were murdered at Rancho San Juan Capistrano, about 45 miles north of San Luis Obispo, and the wife of one was kidnapped. This time, however, the robbers did not adhere to their maxim that "dead men tell no tales," leaving alive the household's two Californio servants.

The next day, in the company of San Luis Obispo's sheriff, the servants identified one of their assailants. The man, known to be a member of a famed band of horse-runners, was taken to jail, where he denied his guilt. He gave an alibi, which was "immediately proved to be false," writes Murray, and was furthermore found to possess some of the dead men's clothes.

That night, a group of citizens barged into the jail and hanged him.

Murray continues to write of an array of crimes in which Pio Linares and "Huero" Rafael were involved. He writes of how citizens set fire to the roof of Linares' home, from which Linares escaped, and of how they tracked down and sometimes shot, sometimes tried and hanged, at least half a dozen criminals, Linares and Rafael among them. Many had been involved in the Rancho San Juan Capistrano incident.

At the beginning, Murray laments, the native Californios did not take part in the Vigilance Committee. But in time, Judge Romualdo Pacheco, a native, stepped in and rallied the Californios to help. Murray praised Pacheco and the Californios in his writings, noting that "being the best horsemen, they are the men who can do more in a chase than any of us."

Pacheco's role in the Vigilance Committee was a great boost to his political career, according to local historian and author Loren Nicholson. Pacheco, having served out a four-year term of judge, planned to run for state senator. His help with the Vigilance Committee, said Nicholson, was at least partly responsible for his successful bid as senator and later elections as state treasurer, lieutenant governor and U.S. congressman.

**A lightly guarded wagon entering a narrow pass was an inviting target for marauding gangs. Holdups and murders incurred the wrath of the vigilantes.**

*Photo/Santa Maria Valley Historical Society*

"Having led a group in the capture of a bandit," said Nicholson, "he was very much a hero among Americans as well as the Californios."

With the support of Pacheco and the Californios, Murray writes, the native residents were less inclined to screen the fugitives in their flight from the committee. It was not long before the Vigilance Committee grew substantially. "Every rogue that is taken and hung," writes Murray, "brings an accession of from twenty to thirty more names to the Vigilance Roll."

The result was a county in which "men walk about unarmed—transact their business and feel at their ease." In time, he added, the horses that had been kept in town, ready to lend chase at a moment's notice, were returned to their own stables.

Not all approved of the committee, however. A Spanish paper in Los Angeles, *El Clamor Publico*, and the *San Francisco Herald* accused the Vigilance Committee of "hasty action and executing men without evidence." Murray answered that the committee had ample evidence for each execution, and was fully justified as a means for the survival of honest citizens of San Luis Obispo County.

"Here, as in San Francisco," he wrote, "I am confident that the law will hereafter work all the better for the quickening spirit infused into it by vigilance."

Apparently he was right. The Vigilance Committee was active for as long as it was needed—a few years at most—then faded quietly away, replaced by a legal system that found new strength and impetus to bring criminals to justice.

Whether or not the Central Coast had more than its share of vigilantes is unknown. Nicholson pointed out that San Francisco had a large and active vigilance group following the Gold Rush of 1849.

"But as you read other county histories," Nicholson said, "you don't run into much of the vigilante idea. I tend to think that our area had more than most. We had a vigilante committee that lasted for awhile, whereas in other areas they may have raised one to chase a group of bandits, then dispersed."

Indeed, times have changed from the days when, according to *History of San Luis Obispo County*, San Luis Obispo was a town where "a bandit once rode through Monterey Street with the ears of his victims tied like scalps to his saddle-bow."

The Central Coast may be more crowded now, but it is also more peaceful—due, at least in part, to the Vigilance Committee of 1858.

*By January Anderson, April 1989*

*The Vigilance Committee was active for as long as it was needed—a few years at most—then faded quietly away*

**M**ARINERS HAVE long dreaded the Central Coast for the fury of its ocean waves, robust winds, treacherous currents and jagged rocks.

Early Spanish explorers and traders christened the Honda Point region, now part of Vandenberg Air Force Base, *La Guijada del Diablo* meaning "The Devil's Jaw." Historians have dubbed the coastline between Point Arguello and Point Purisima the "Graveyard of Ships" because of the many wrecks that have occurred there.

During the California Gold Rush era, passenger ship traffic along the Central Coast increased as adventurers journeyed to and from the booming San Francisco and Sacramento areas. With the growing traffic came shipwrecks made more disastrous because of the antics of gold-fevered passengers and crews.

An early Gold Rush era shipwreck occurred in August 1848 when the steamship *Edith*, filled with prospective gold miners headed for San Francisco via Cape Horn at the tip of South America, ran aground at Honda Point after becoming trapped in a treacherous current. The ship was not greatly damaged but still wound up a total loss.

Historians reveal that the crew deliberately wrecked the *Edith* so they could abandon her and head for the gold mines. William Goodman Dana, a pioneer settler of the Nipomo area, is credited with salvaging from the *Edith's* wreckage an intact round wooden table that can be seen today in the San Luis Obispo Historical Society Museum.

The December 1853 sinking of the sidewheeler *Winfield Scott* on her voyage from San Francisco to Panama also involved gold miners—this time successful miners returning to the East Coast with their fortunes.

When the *Winfield Scott* reached the northern end of the Santa Barbara Channel at about 2 a.m. on December 4, fog so heavy "you could almost cut it with a knife," according to survivors, prevented the ship's officers from realizing that they had drifted off course. The ship ran ashore at Anacapa Island and was pushed onto rocks by the pounding surf.

In an account given to the *Ventura Free Press* by one of the surviving passengers, F.S. Crane of Sycamore, IL, readers learned how the ship's captain and first mate stood over the lifeboats with drawn revolvers to prevent the panic-stricken passengers from commandeering them.

The captain sent one lifeboat with four crew members ashore to scout for a safe landing place. All of the lifeboats were then lowered and the passengers transferred to shore, but not before two male passengers were caught stealing from other passengers' treasure-laden bags. The two thieves were placed in irons, stripped and flogged. The severe public whipping had the desired effect of eliminating further undesirable behavior.

When daylight arrived and the fog lifted, the crew and passengers realized they were on a large rock near the main island. Once again, the lifeboats were used, this time to

# Lost Souls in the 'Graveyard of Ships'

shuttle everyone to a safer place on Anacapa Island. Then the captain and crew painstakingly loaded the ship's cargo of $2 million in gold bullion, mail and baggage onto the lifeboats for transfer to the island. An armed guard was placed over these items for the duration of the stay, which ended five days later when the passengers were rescued by boats from two passing ships.

Gold fever also played a part in the wreck of the sidewheeler *Yankee Blade* in 1854. When the ship, filled with gold and miners heading to Panama, departed from San Francisco on September 29 along with three other steamers—the *Sonora*, the *Cortez*, and the *Goliah*—a rumor circulated about a $5000 wager between the captains as to which ship would reach Panama first.

About 24 hours into the voyage, the steamers encountered dense fog along the coast. Capt. Henry Randall of the *Yankee Blade* did not slow down or check the depth of the water near Point Arguello, believing he was further south than he really was.

Suddenly the crew and passengers were thrown off their feet by a tremendous jolt. There was a grinding sound as the *Yankee Blade* was ripped by rocks about three quarters of a mile offshore. The bow tilted upward onto a rock; the stern went under water.

Seventeen people died during the rescue operations, some when lifeboats overturned in thundering breakers and some when their heavy gold mining belts dragged them under. The ship's officers transported about 150 passengers to shore by nightfall; the rest stayed aboard the tottering ship the rest of the night.

Since Randall and most of his officers were on the beach with the rescued passengers, the crew that remained on board abandoned all semblance of order and discipline. Together with a group of rowdies from the steerage class, they turned that night into a double nightmare for the rest of the passengers, terrorizing them with knives and guns and looting the first-class cabins. They also broke into the ship's liquor stores and spent the night consuming the treasure they found there. Probably the liquor helped dampen their disappointment at not being able to reach the immense gold bullion shipment which was in a part of the ship already under water.

The next morning the *Goliah*, which had wisely slowed the previous evening when it encountered the fog, reached the wreck and launched lifeboats to rescue the frantic *Yankee Blade* passengers, bringing them to San Pedro.

Those *Yankee Blade* passengers still onshore spent a traumatic week awaiting the *Goliah's* return. A group of crew members and steerage rogues repeatedly beat and robbed them, then tried to sell the stolen goods back to the same passengers at exorbitant prices. Needless to say, they were ecstatic when the *Goliah* returned on October 8.

In the maritime inquiry that followed, Randall was criticized for running the ship so close to shore and for lack

*Gold fever also played a part in the wreck of the sidewheeler* Yankee Blade *in 1854*

of control over the marauding crew and passengers. But no punitive action was taken, much to the dismay of the victims and the shocked public.

In 1856 the *Santa Barbara Gazette* reported that Randall, now captain of the schooner *Ada*, had salvaged the sunken treasure. The *Yankee Blade's* ex-captain enlisted the help of Navy divers during his salvage operation, and he slipped away without returning the gold to its rightful owners.

An interesting historical aside to the *Yankee Blade* incident: Charles Haskell Clark, one of the pioneer developers of the Santa Maria Valley, is said in the book *This Is Our Valley* to have salvaged wood from the *Yankee Blade*. Clark used the lumber to build his family's home at Point Sal, thus preserving a bit of Gold Rush adventure and tragedy on the Central Coast.

*By Melissa Abramovitz, September 1991*

**The *Yankee Blade* was one of many Gold Rush-era vessels to run aground near Point Arguello.**

# The Forgotten Town of La Graciosa

I N SPANISH, *La Graciosa* means "the graceful" or "beautiful" or "pleasing."

And to Spanish explorers two centuries ago, the southwestern portion of the Santa Maria Valley must have been pleasing to the senses, with its mild climate, gracefully rolling hills, lagoon and thickets of willows. The diaries of several explorers refer to the region as "La Graciosa."

The lyrical La Graciosa was the name given to one of the earliest settlements in northern Santa Barbara County. In 1868, long before there was a Lompoc or Central City (now Santa Maria), there was La Graciosa.

But ask any longtime resident of these parts about La Graciosa, and he or she is bound to reply "Yeah, that place" while pointing in the general direction of Orcutt.

The exact site is subject to debate. The best estimate is that the town grew near the spot where the Orcutt Expressway (South Broadway) curves toward Highway 1 south of Clark Avenue, just a stone's throw from some Unocal storage tanks. Some think the freeway runs directly over the ruins of La Graciosa.

Finding out anything else about La Graciosa requires a great deal of digging. The community rose and fell in 10 years and virtually vanished in the aftermath of a giant land deal.

The history comes in snatches from old-timers with good memories and dusty county records. When pieced together, they tell much about an early seed of civilization on the Central Coast.

Hardy wanderers from Santa Cruz began to arrive in the hills near present-day Orcutt around 1864, but many were chased from the promising land by droughts.

The sturdy stuck it out. One was Don Patricio O'Neill, an Irish soldier in exile who around 1868 established La Graciosa by opening a store and saloon on the site.

"I asked my uncle once where it was built," recalled Chet Norris of Orcutt, "and he pointed out a spring with some willows. They always located first near water."

The saloon was also a part-time courtroom, and judges of the court of La Graciosa had jurisdiction from the Santa Maria River to Santa Barbara.

One tale recounts how a member of the Arellanes family sauntered into the saloon and ordered a drink while an inquest was in progress. The magistrate, a man named Green, immediately fined Arellanes $5 for contempt but set aside the fine on condition that he buy a round for the crowd.

La Graciosa was a rough little hamlet—like so many during that period in the West. It was the location of the Santa Maria Valley's first two homicides, both shootings, one between drinkers in the saloon and the other between arguing cattlemen, or so the story goes.

But La Graciosa also had the valley's first school district and post office. According to Earl Jennings of Orcutt, the store, post office and school shared the same building with a stage station.

O'Neill wanted to accommodate a run by the Coast Line Stage Company between the new settlements at Guadalupe and Los Alamos. One volume of historical record states: "The stage was held up many times south of La Graciosa, and many people believed that the postmaster stood in with the bandits."

Later La Graciosa was part of the route for the narrow gauge Pacific Coast Railway.

By most accounts, the saloon and stage/store/post office/school building were the only substantial structures in La Graciosa. They were surrounded by shanties.

La Graciosa was the trading and social center for the settlers who found water on government land to the north and northeast. They turned the small valleys into orchards with hundreds of acres of peach, plum, nectarine, walnut and orange trees. As walnut trees grew to the prodigious height of 10 feet in two years, the farmers dubbed the area "Fruitvale."

But a few dry years shriveled the fruit, and Fruitvale passed from memory.

The settlers remained, however, and their names are now important names in Santa Maria Valley history: Brookshire, Stubblefield, Marcum, Holloway, Righetti, Twitchell, Haslam and others.

By the late 1870s a voting district, called La Graciosa, had been established. In 1876 the Town Company surveyed 40 lots with plans to sell them and create a full-fledged town.

Standing in the way was Henry Mayo Newhall, railroad and cattle baron. Newhall had received title to a portion of the sprawling Todos Santos Rancho, and La Graciosa stood on the extreme northern limit of his property.

From there history "gets murky and hazy and kind of confused," said Bob Woods of Santa Maria, a descendant of the Newhall family. "Nothing has been substantiated."

The most reliable record is an editorial from the *Guadalupe Telegraph* dated January 27, 1877:

"Goodbye, La Graciosa. We understand the little town is soon to be effaced from the map of our county. H.M. Newhall has had the land on which it stands confirmed to him and he has served suits of ejection on all the inhabitants, besides claiming some $40,000 in damages.

"We sympathize with our unlucky neighbors, but such is life among the Spanish grants."

The squatters' shacks were torn or burned down. Deane Walker of Orcutt recalled his father telling how he "moved two buildings into (what became) the town of Orcutt. It was a matter of one-half mile he had to move them. As time passes I haven't been able to tell exactly where the buildings sat."

The dismantling of La Graciosa was so complete that within a few years the site became a subject of folklore.

There was a short-lived "New Graciosa" supposedly populated by the evicted squatters. And Graciosa later became the name of a railroad siding, oil company, oil workers camp and a ridge in the oil-drilling region south of Orcutt.

*La Graciosa was the trading and social center for the settlers who found water on government land to the north and northeast*

Recalled Ivan "Hap" Worsham of Orcutt: "When Union Oil put tanks over there they did a heckuva lot of bulldozing. Several people went digging out there and found old, rusted-out pistols, cooking utensils and other things left around."

But that was decades ago. Today there is only Graciosa Road, the frontage road that parallels Highway 1/S-20 on its way to Vandenberg Air Force Base.

Yet there remains an ode to La Graciosa, composed by a poet/settler, John McPherson, who it appears was smitten by the graceful land ...

> Graciosa! Graciosa! thy name,
> when uttered by a Spanish maiden,
> sounds like a drop of liquid silver
> falling upon a bed of roses.

*By Bob Nelson, January 1986*

MAIN AND BROADWAY, Santa Maria, 1984—the heart of the Central Coast's commercial hub, bounded by two banks, a gas station and an apartment complex.

Main and Broadway, 1869—emptiness. No streets, no buildings, no one to call it home. Just another wind-whipped point in an unforgiving, desert-like valley.

Between then and now came John Thornburg, Isaac Fesler, Isaac Miller and Rudolph Cook. These immigrants wrought a miracle of sorts—creating a city at Main and Broadway without planners, building permits, environmental impact reports or other government interference.

But perhaps a century ago the uncomplicated birth of a city was not so miraculous.

"Similar things were happening in the western movement," said Phillip Ault, a relative of the Thornburg family and a chronicler of Santa Maria history.

"A cluster of people would get together and organize and put down some streets," Ault explained, "and other people would crowd to it. I imagine the same happened here."

It happened long after the establishment of Santa Barbara and San Luis Obispo, huddled around missions. In the early 1800s the Santa Maria Valley was a treeless wasteland surrounded by huge ranchos formed during the Mexican land grant period.

"Apparently the Mexican politicians couldn't even give the (valley) land away," Ault said. "When it became federal land (after the Mexican-American and Civil wars), it was open to homesteading."

The Homestead Act allowed pioneers to claim a 160-acre parcel of land, build a home, plant a crop and call the land their own after five years. And there was land for the taking in the Santa Maria Valley.

Rudolph Cook came in 1869, via Quincy, Illinois and the gold fields and ranches of Northern California. He brought lumber from Port Harford (now Port San Luis) to construct a two-room, two-story home on what is now the corner of Main and McClelland streets.

Isaac Fesler soon arrived by way of Missouri and Northern California. He wanted to farm, and his watermelons were good enough to win prizes at local fairs.

John Thornburgh came in 1871 from the Midwest, 62 years of age and suffering terribly from asthma. He eventually dropped the last letter of his name and picked up the title of "Uncle" and "Grandpa" as a patriarch to both elders and youngsters.

Isaac Miller saw something of value in the area in 1873 and staked his claim. He is considered the first to plant fruit trees.

Each owned an adjoining quarter section of a square mile of the flattest, dustiest part of the valley floor—Cook on the southeast, Miller on the northeast, Fesler on the northwest and Thornburg on the southwest.

# Santa Maria's Founding Fathers

For the pioneers, life was an endurance test.

"It was an empty land, barren, with no trees—nothing to block the wind," said Ault. "In the spring there would be constant dust and wind, and it was dry six months of the year.

"Coyotes raided the chicken coops. Wild horses destroyed crops. There were grasshoppers and grass fires."

Water came by barrel from Suey Crossing at the Santa Maria River, a long haul. The nearest outpost was the farm town of Guadalupe.

"There was nothing here," Ault said, "to attract people."

But by 1874 a dozen families had been attracted and some homes and businesses built, and Cook, Fesler, Miller and Thornburg decided the time had come to lay out a townsite. Ault figured they probably shook hands on the decision over the counter of Thornburg's small Grange store.

City-creating was equally simple. Each landowner contributed 40 acres where their properties joined, now the four corners at the intersection of Main and Broadway.

They commissioned a survey of the proposed townsite, registered it with the county, printed maps ... and were suddenly city fathers. They named their offspring Central City.

"It was as unlike a contemporary planned development as was humanly possible to do," Ault said.

Unplanned maybe, but not unwise. The founders showed the foresight to set aside enough land to form the 120-foot-wide Broadway. The spacious street helped when turning their unwieldy horse-drawn wagons; today it smooths the flow of automobile traffic.

Within a decade, the seed planted at the four corners was growing larger than Guadalupe. An 80-foot well was dug to pipe water into every home; 40,000 newly planted eucalyptus trees broke the wind; the Pacific Coast Railway arrived; the once-arid area was promoted as "The Valley of Gardens."

And what of Cook, Miller, Fesler and Thornburg? They faded into history, although their names are immortalized on street signs that dissect the land they furnished to create a city.

*By Bob Nelson, November 1984*

*Each landowner contributed 40 acres where their properties joined, now the four corners at the intersection of Main and Broadway*

## LOMPOC VALLEY LAND COMPANY.

$550 00

Assessment No. 1
Levied _____ 187 }

San Jose Oct 29th 1874

Received from _Andrew L Huyck_ the sum a Check payable to National Gold Bank & Trust Co. Treas Lompoc valley Land Co. of _Five Hundred & Fifty ($551 00)_ Dollars, being Assessment No. 1 of 11 per cent per Share, on _One_ Shares of the Capital Stock of the above named Company, standing in the name of _Andrew L Huyck_ on the Company's Books.

Certif. No. _____

George Roberts

By _Henry Phelps_

SECRETARY.

---

**D**URING THE 19TH century, the West gave birth to hundreds of small towns for hundreds of reasons: gold in California, silver in Nevada, free land for cattle grazing in Montana and Texas, new railroad lines in Kansas and Arizona, religious freedom in Utah.

In Lompoc, California, it was temperance. Temperance, "the moderation in or abstinence from the use of intoxicating drink," according to *Webster's Dictionary*. Plenty of folks fought for temperance during that era, but few thought of making temperance the purpose for establishing a community.

The founders of Lompoc did, and the idea caught on so well that in 1874 the Lompoc Valley was the scene of one of those legendary, wild Old West land rushes of settlers seeking prosperity and sobriety.

It was the brainchild of W.W. Broughton of Santa Cruz, newspaper editor and devoted advocate of the temperance cause. He sought land in Southern California where he could create a settlement for people with similar views.

During an 1870 business trip to Santa Barbara, Broughton passed through a coastal valley that contained the sprawling Lompoc Rancho and Mission Viejo de la Purisima Rancho, both Mexican land grants owned by Americans but inhabited almost entirely by sheep, cattle and horses. "There, for the first time, Broughton beheld the beautiful vista of Lompoc Valley, carpeted with yellow mustard and green trees and walled by wooded hills," a native, Myra Manfrina, told the *Lompoc Record* in 1956. The land was fertile and supplied with enough water to support thousands of people.

**The idea of a town devoted to the temperance cause attracted investors like Mr. Huyck to the Lompoc Valley Land Company in 1874.**
*Courtesy Lompoc Valley Historical Society*

# THE GREAT LOMPOC LAND RUSH

"His imagination began working immediately," she said, "and then and there he envisioned the colonization of the great ranchos."

Four years later Broughton formed the Lompoc Valley Land Company and, with capital provided by businessmen from San Francisco, Santa Barbara and Santa Cruz, bought the Lompoc and Mission Viejo ranchos. By November 1874, promotion of the Lompoc Colony and its no-liquor standards had attracted dozens of families to the valley.

Surveyors for Broughton and the Land Company divided the property into lots of five, 10, 20, 40 and 80 acres with a one-square-mile plot nine miles from the ocean reserved for a townsite. "For days before the time of the sale, the ground was alive with people on the lookout for homesites ... many brought seeds and farming utensils all set to go to work," Manfrina said. Most settlers were from California, but the the news of Lompoc's temperance community also attracted people from Ohio, Kentucky, Indiana and Missouri.

On November 9, the land rush exploded.

Said Manfrina: "It could be likened to the pack of hounds after the fox—excitement was high! The bidders—250 men and 20 women—descended upon the valley in an odd assortment of vehicles—four and two-horse stages, wagons of all descriptions, buggies, horseback and muleback. They raced about pell-mell over the land in a great cloud of dust."

Broughton led the crowd, joined by an auctioneer who rushed from one location to another, waving a red flag and completing sales. He was followed "by the whole cavalcade and caravan, all driving or riding like mad, and each striving to outstrip his fellows," according to one chronicler.

The first lot sold for the princely sum of $705; after four days the land company had disposed of 11,000 acres at an average price of $60 an acre, much higher than the value of public land elsewhere in Santa Barbara County. "Such a sale of wild land is utterly unprecedented," W.H. Martin wrote in the *Santa Barbara Press*.

Five days later, the *Press* reported that "a dozen buildings are now under way, for which lumber was taken over from Point Sal Landing, and families are camping on the ground waiting the construction of dwellings.

"It will be a colony of just such people as we need in Santa Barbara County," the story went on, "sober, industrious, well-to-do farmers who are seeking permanent homes, and cannot, certainly, be suspected of the faintest desire to speculate, when they pay such prices to begin with."

Sobriety was the common bond for most new residents. The bylaws of the Lompoc Land Company were explicit: "No vinous, malt, spiritous or other intoxicating liquors shall be manufactured or sold upon any portion of the Lompoc and Mission Viejo Ranchos purchased by this corporation ..." Absolute temperance was a condition included in every deed of sale.

But "temperance was hard to control," noted Anne Calvert, a Lompoc history devotee. "The stagecoach came in,

*'It could be likened to the pack of hounds after the fox —excitement was high!'*

and on every stage there were people with some bottles."

And nearby Los Alamos became an oasis for those who found Lompoc's anti-liquor laws restrictive. Over the years, tiny Los Alamos contained as many as seven saloons.

During that first year, though, few Lompocans gave liquor a passing thought. There was too much work to be done, homes to be erected, roads to be constructed, land to be cleared, a wharf to be completed.

"A lot of people lived in tents that first year," Calvert said, "and a lot of little buildings were hurriedly put up. It's interesting that for a whole year no one died. You would think some of them would have died of pneumonia, which was a very serious thing at that time. Apparently they were a very healthy group."

Decades later, pioneer Will Robinson recalled life with his father in a log cabin, circa 1875: "I never knew what a pair of stockings, boots or shoes were for four years. We had no watch or clock, and father would make me get out of a warm bed to see if I could see the morning star over the mountains south of the cabin. If I could, I had to dress and go after the horses. The vegetation was often covered with heavy frost which was like ice, and being barefooted the grass and ice would cut my feet, making them bleed."

When Lompoc celebrated its first anniversary in November 1875, the colony contained 200 families, a school district with 225 students, churches, a newspaper (edited by Broughton), a physician, justice of the peace, a blacksmith and a smattering of merchants. It was to be the last good year for quite a while.

*When Lompoc celebrated its first anniversary in November 1875, the colony contained 200 families*

In 1876, land values dropped and the barely completed wharf on the beach west of town washed away. The next year brought one of the most severe droughts on record; thousands of cattle and sheep died and hunger was a real threat for many Lompocans. In 1878, a diphtheria epidemic killed many children.

The Lompoc Land Company ran into difficulty. After the monumental first land rush, fewer and fewer settlers came to the valley. Land prices plummeted. The board of directors missed a $50,000 payment due the original owners of the ranchos.

In October 1879, the original owners reacquired most of the unsold property, and the Lompoc Land Company quietly passed into history.

Many Old West towns, struck by a similar string of calamities, dried up and blew away. Not Lompoc. The soil was still fertile, the water good, and the knot of temperance bound the community. Cityhood was proclaimed on August 13, 1888.

Temperance? It barely outlasted the city's incorporation. But drinkers in any new saloon tended to look warily over their shoulders for the followers of W.W. Broughton.

*By Bob Nelson, January 1988*

*Up there you aren't bothered by people too much, and that was fine with me.*

**—Adrian Davis on growing up in the Manzana region**

# Homesteaders in the Wilderness

IN THE SUMMER of 1985 Jim Morrow hiked and camped in the wildly scenic area often referred to as "The Manzana"—a portion of the Los Padres National Forest east of Santa Maria coursed by the Sisquoc and Manzana rivers.

The rivers were rather dry that summer when Morrow, an Allan Hancock College instructor and naturalist, searched for the remains of century-old pioneer settlements that occupied the few flatlands in an otherwise rocky, jumbled terrain.

He found mostly debris, some stone chimneys and fireplaces, farm implements and barbed wire. "I couldn't find several sites," he said later. "They must have been overgrown by chaparral.

"Except for the Tunnell house, it's pretty much just rubble and ruin."

The two-story Tunnell house, constructed of pine and sturdy sycamore, withstood the decades, as did the schoolhouse that once served as an education/social center and a pioneer cabin. Each has been designated a Santa Barbara County historical landmark.

They are relics of the 19th-century thrust of the homestead movement in California.

Congress passed the Homestead Act of 1862 to speed settlement of the nation's vast western territories and states. The gist of the law was that the head of a family could claim 160 acres of open land and take title to it by building a home and farming the land for five years.

In 1868 six homesteading families staked out their claims in the Santa Maria Valley. The Tunnells, with eight sons and two daughters, settled on land that now includes Allan Hancock College.

The family made a go of it in the wind-whipped valley, but by the time the children had grown up there were only slim pickings of land suitable for homesteading.

In 1885, 20-year-old George Tunnell and his brother Henry packed their belongings and moved up the Sisquoc River where another brother, Will, had brought his young family.

They sought to "find a spot in the canyons with a few good acres," said Curtis Tunnell, George's son and a former county supervisor and Santa Maria mayor. "They were looking for a little land where they could farm a patch of hay and have a few fruit trees and gardens. And there were a few side hills that weren't entirely covered with brush, so they could graze some cattle."

The Tunnell boys settled near the river within a few miles of Will. There were other families named Davis, Wheat, Forrester, Wells, Twitchell, Montgomery, Abel, Whitney,

Boyer among others, all strung out along 20 miles of the Sisquoc and Manzana.

Their homes had bare floors, were heated by fireplaces and wood-burning stoves and lit by coal-oil lamps. Will Tunnell's two-story home, with floors hewn from sycamore, was an exception.

Some water came from wells, the rest was hauled in barrels from the river.

Before long there was a sawmill and school that accommodated as many as 25 students and served as a dance hall.

"It was a pretty tough existence," said Curtis Tunnell.

The homesteaders lived on whatever they could scratch from the earth—potatoes, apples, beans, melons—and their livestock. Most arable land was devoted to growing hay, the fuel for cattle, hogs and sometimes sheep.

"You couldn't live up there if you didn't have a cow ... to get a little milk and make a little butter," added Tunnell.

The Tunnells milked "a range cow, not a 'bossy'-in-the-backyard cow. Those range cattle running in the hills were pretty spooky, and they would not let you milk them without a fight.

"You had to tie it to a post and pull it up good and tight, then pick up one of its hind feet so it couldn't kick you. Then you could take a bucket and put it under her and milk her. She wouldn't like it, but she couldn't do anything about it."

Periodically the settlers would make the long, difficult trek to Santa Maria to sell or trade their livestock and produce for necessities—flour, sugar, salt and pepper, coffee, clothing.

**Cowboys from the sprawling Sisquoc Ranch used the old Tunnell home as a way station in the wilderness.**

*Photo/Santa Maria Valley Historical Society*

"They never knew what money was, but they didn't need as much," Tunnell said. "If they had a few silver dollars in their pocket they were well fixed."

Back at the ranch, families lived in splendid isolation, miles from their neighbors. In winter they were often cut off from the outside world when heavy rains made the rivers tumble and roar.

Occasionally the solitude was interrupted by adventures. The younger Tunnell remembers being told how the homesteaders formed a posse and tracked and captured a horse thief deep in the high-country wilderness.

Another time a grizzly bear "raised hell with a couple of places, killed the livestock" he said. "The fellows got together and tracked that bear down and killed it. It was not an easy thing. You had better be sure your aim was straight."

After 18 years George Tunnell, still unmarried, left the area. It was part of an exodus that began with the closing of the Manzana schoolhouse in 1903.

Robert E. Easton, a civil engineer surveying the sprawling Sisquoc land grant, placed the boundary of the grant about a quarter mile north of its original position—overlapping into some homestead lands.

At first angered, the settlers later sold their lands to the Sisquoc Ranch for $5 an acre. The sturdy Tunnell home was for decades an outpost for ranch cowboys.

One of the last to leave the region was Adrian Davis. He moved there with his family at a tender age. They lived near the old saw mill; his father worked for the U.S. Forest Service and ran some cattle.

"We got along pretty good," he said later, "except it could get awful cold in the winter. Sometimes it snowed."

Davis hunted and fished, "and I'd go help work on a trail someplace or help build fence. There was always something to do."

In the summer a game warden from Santa Maria would bring his family to the mountains to join the Davis kids in fishing, hiking, "and we'd go swimming in the creek. There were some nice holes to swim in."

Davis left the area at about age nine to go to school. The region has changed little since he left; no electricity or telephones or plumbing, just the vestiges of the homesteading era.

*By Bob Nelson, April 1987*

*Families lived in splendid isolation, miles from their neighbors*

O N THE SEAWARD face of the Santa Ynez Mountains, autos from Santa Barbara race up Highway 154 to San Marcos Pass and its 15-mile shortcut to the Central Coast.

Within earshot of the stream of traffic is a stretch of hand-hewn roadway in the bedrock that is overgrown with mesquite and chaparral—"Slippery Rock." A century ago it was known to stagecoach drivers as "Slippery Sal," a particularly treacherous spot on the twisting grade that offered the best link between the coast and the interior.

The stage's six horses or mules struggled up the steep stone trail scarred with lateral cuts to provide footing. The driver manhandled his team to keep the stage wheels running in the deep grooves chopped out of the rock— tracks designed to provide a margin of safety on the way to the summit.

Slippery Sal was a fearsome mistress, as the *Santa Barbara Press* reported January 18, 1875:

"Just above Slippery Rock ... a landslide occurred which frightened one of the leading horses. The plunging horse fell over the bank, carrying his mate with him. As they fell the other horses braced themselves and held on, thus saving the stage from going over. The driver, to save the balance of the team, cut loose the leaders and they rolled about 200 feet down the mountain."

Such was life on the transportation system that connected the sparsely populated Central Coast to the outside world, a rutted lifeline sometimes disconnected by storms and harried by highwaymen. Stage service lasted in various forms for four decades, long after railroads—even autos—made the stagecoach a relic elsewhere in the West.

In the 1850s the rich new state of California goaded the federal government for better mail service. Officials decided on regular stage service to replace the haphazard runs of coastal steamships and lone horsemen.

Stages already served booming San Francisco and Sacramento, also Los Angeles, a sleepy town of 1600 whose potential inspired eastern promoters and speculators. But how to deliver the mail between north and south?

Into the void stepped the Overland Mail Company. The stage line obtained a government contract in March 1861 to transport the mail three times a week between San Francisco and Los Angeles.

The route was to tie Monterey, San Antonio, San Luis Obispo and Santa Barbara to the Southland, and the contract stipulated that mail be delivered with "certainty, celerity and security."

On April 1 the first Overland stage rolled into Santa Barbara to the cheers of the populace and completed the San Francisco-to-Los Angeles coast connection in an amazing—for then—72 hours.

Overland used the Concord stagecoach, built in Massachusetts to accommodate 21 passengers—12 in roof-top

# The Golden Age of the Stagecoach

**Driven by John Waugh, a stagecoach crosses the rain-swollen Santa Ynez River.**

*Photo/Santa Maria Valley Historical Society*

seats. Leather-covered racks, called "boots," hung at the front and rear to hold mail and baggage; a compartment under the driver's seat held the treasure box.

The one-ton vehicle was fitted with springs made of bullhide to cushion the ride. Still, the Concord proved too frail for the rugged coast route and was replaced by coaches bearing the name of the West's premier banking and express company, Wells Fargo.

Blacksmith shops were erected at 15-mile intervals to service stages and teams.

After leaving Monterey, the stage rambled through the plains to the east of the coastal mountains before descending into San Luis Obispo. Next stop was the Dana Adobe in present-day Nipomo.

Santa Maria did not exist when the first stage arrived. It forded the Santa Maria River at the Suey Crossing and traversed the valley to Rancho Tinaquaic in Foxen Canyon.

Following the present Foxen Canyon Road to what is now Ballard, the stage veered west to Mission Santa Inez and headed toward the coast at Gaviota Pass.

In his *History of Santa Barbara County*, Owen O'Neill described the trail:

"At Gaviota the fissure allowing passage through the sandstone ridge along the coast was little more than wide enough to let a wagon through; thence the road led up a wild and rocky canyon."

When heavy rains washed out the roadbed at Gaviota Pass, stages occasionally were lowered by ropes over the precipices.

That procedure would never do. Los Angeles howled about delays in mail deliveries. A group of Santa Barbara entrepreneurs in 1868 divined a profitable solution—a shorter and, presumably, safer toll road over the mountains near what is now San Marcos Pass.

Pioneer Benjamin Foxen was recruited to retrace the trail over San Marcos Pass where, 20 years earlier, he had led John C. Fremont during his campaign to conquer California for America. Chinese road gangs—using picks, axes and blasting powder—completed the project.

In 1869 the Santa Ynez Turnpike Road opened (with Foxen, it is said, driving the first team over the pass). Tolls as high as $2.50 for a vehicle and four horses were collected at the pass while passengers ate at Patrick Kinevan's "summit house" or the nearby Cold Spring Tavern—still serving today.

By that time other stage firms had replaced Overland. New routes connected the established communities in northern Santa Barbara County—Guadalupe, La Graciosa (near present-day Orcutt) and Los Alamos.

For 15 years mail and passengers rolled over the toll road. Certainty and celerity were impossible to guarantee, however.

The pounding of hooves and the rattle of gear on rugged sections of the road—like Slippery Rock—were constant annoyances. With its high profile, the stage rocked and swayed as it rounded sharp mountain turns at high speed, giving tourists a heart-in-your-throat view of the mountainside.

At several spots along the route, where the road narrowed to a few feet and going over the edge meant a drop of 1000 feet, passengers were encouraged "to alight to take a view and stretch their legs by walking a mile or so," O'Neill reported. Most passengers took the suggestion.

The road often vanished during a storm, or the adobe soil became so sticky that coach wheels warped and broke. At such times a horseback rider with a shovel accompanied the stage to keep the wheels clean.

These were among the obstacles overcome by drivers, or "whips," such as John Waugh, who ferried passengers in the 1870s. He was typical of the drivers who came to the coast after railroads forced them out of work in the mining country to the north. They were masters at manipulating the brake as well as master storytellers during dull hours on the trail.

Recalled Waugh: "If the stage was running by night, the two lanterns in front up over the wheelers would be lighted, and they would throw a little beam ahead, though not much of one. You had to leave a good deal of it to the horses, and the road was rough. If there was rain, so much the worse."

Security was breached by robbers, well-known highwaymen like Jack Powers and Joaquin Murietta and nameless bandits who preyed on stages slowing to navigate a narrow or steep stretch of road. Waugh's stage never carried a guard, and drivers were instructed never to

*The road often vanished during a storm, or the adobe soil became so sticky that coach wheels warped and broke*

fight—a gunshot might spook the horses and cause an accident.

In *This Is Our Valley*, rancher Diego Villa described two holdups:

"The robber got away with the strong box. He had placed two dummies—one on each side of the road—with pointed sticks instead of guns, and when the stage came along he shouted to his dummies not to shoot until he gave the order, and he proceeded to stick up the stage.

"In 1880 two stages were robbed at the foot of San Marcos Pass. A stage going north and one going south were robbed at about the same time. One lady being robbed complained that the robber was taking all her money, so he returned some of it to her."

Wells Fargo's first solution was to fasten the strong box to an iron ring built into the stage. This forced the bandits to double up; one stood guard over the passengers while the other smashed the box loose or emptied it on the spot.

Organized gangs brought the wave of holdups to a peak in 1870. Wells Fargo offered a $750 reward for a loss of $1000.

Honest townspeople sought protection in additional lawmen and in vigilance committees. Several hangings curtailed but never eliminated the problem.

*By the mid-1880s the railroad was a greater menace to the stagecoach than the highwayman*

By the mid-1880s the railroad was a greater menace to the stagecoach than the highwayman. The Southern Pacific had reached San Luis Obispo from the north and Santa Barbara from the south, and the narrow-gauge Pacific Coast Railway connected communities from San Luis Obispo to Los Olivos.

The lone gap between north and south was the 40 miles between Los Olivos and Santa Barbara over San Marcos Pass. The stage filled the gap.

In 1886 Felix Mattei built a combination stage office, hotel and restaurant along the railroad siding in Los Olivos. Rail passengers could rest overnight for the six-hour stage ride to Santa Barbara. The fare was $5.50.

Mattei could claim that the last commercial stagecoach line in western history ended its run at Mattei's Tavern. Even after the Southern Pacific completed its coast line in 1901, Mattei owned a small branch stage line to carry mail between Los Olivos and Gaviota.

The stage ran until 1912 when it was replaced by a Model T Ford.

One hundred years after their golden age, stagecoaches are among two dozen Old West vehicles preserved in the Carriage House at the Santa Ynez Valley Historical Society Museum.

Parked neatly in rows, the carriages retain a certain stateliness and grandeur—character forged during decades of encounters with Slippery Sal.

*By Bob Nelson, May 1986*

S OMEONE WITH a sharp eye may notice the indentation of a narrow, long-forgotten trail that cuts through the tawny countryside along the left side of Highway 154 as it turns east from Highway 101, a few miles north of Buellton, and leads to Los Olivos.

Another may spot a few graying boxcars sitting in fields and back country around the San Luis Obispo County Airport, or, resting beneath an orange tree in the front yard of a house near Buchon and Santa Rosa streets in San Luis Obispo, a little rail-wheeled handcart sometimes planted with flowers.

These are a few of the last reminders of the once-thriving Pacific Coast Railway, a narrow-gauge railroad that, in its heyday from the 1880s through the 1920s, hauled lumber, grain, produce, oil, gravel—and people—to and from locations ranging from the wharf at Port San Luis to Los Olivos, taking in San Luis Obispo, Arroyo Grande, Nipomo, Santa Maria, Guadalupe, Betteravia, Los Alamos and the Palmer oil fields a few miles southwest of Sisquoc.

The railway began in 1873 at Port San Luis, then known as Port Harford. That was where entrepreneur John Harford built a horse-drawn railway to carry freight and passengers to and from the flats at San Luis Creek near Avila to the steamships that stopped at Port Harford, where Port San Luis pier now stands.

About a year later, San Francisco steamship line operator Charles Goodall formed the San Luis Obispo and Santa Maria Valley Railroad with the intent of hauling grain, cattle and dairy products from the ranchos in southern San Luis Obispo County to his ships at Port Harford. Plans were to lay rail from San Luis Bay to the Santa Maria River and eventually to Santa Barbara.

The company, led by a board of directors from the San Luis Obispo area, bought Harford's wharf and horse-drawn railroad and rebuilt it to accommodate steam-powered engines. By late summer 1876, two trains were running daily on track laid by Chinese laborers from a station at the corner of South and Higuera streets in San Luis Obispo to Avila.

In 1881 a new company was named after Goodall's Pacific Coast Steamship Co.: the Pacific Coast Railroad, although its officers were the same as those involved with the San Luis Obispo and Santa Maria Valley Railroad. By October, Pacific Coast Railroad track ran from San Luis Obispo through Corbett Canyon to Arroyo Grande, carrying three loads of grain per day to Port Harford.

The Chinese laborers continued to lay track southward, and on April 22, 1882 they reached Santa Maria, then known as Central City.

Meanwhile, the Northern Pacific and the Oregon Railway and Navigation Co. bought controlling interest in the Pacific Coast Steamship Co.—and with it, the San Luis Obispo and Santa Maria Valley Railroad and the Pacific Coast Railroad. It was soon consolidated into one company, the Pacific

# The Pacific Coast Railway Links a Pioneer Domain

Coast Railway.

By October 1882 the Pacific Coast Railway had reached Los Alamos, and a little more than five years later it ended at Los Olivos.

With its advance into each town, the Railway was greeted with great fanfare and celebration. For these were days when long-distance transportation along the West Coast was either by ship or by stagecoach; the Southern Pacific Railroad did not connect San Luis Obispo with San Francisco until 1894, and it was not until 1901 that the Southern Pacific spanned San Francisco to Los Angeles.

In essence, the Pacific Coast Railway opened the door of the Central Coast to the rest of the world. Meat, grain and produce rode the train to Port Harford where ships carried it away to San Francisco and other major ports, bringing back lumber and goods needed by Central Coast pioneers—many of whom also arrived via the same ships and railroad.

At the turn of the century, the Pacific Coast Railway was busy 24 hours a day, hauling grain to Port Harford, unaware of a whole new freight in the ground beneath it—oil. The first big oil wells were drilled in 1901; by 1913 Port Harford was a major West Coast oil shipping port. The oil more than helped replace the dwindling seagoing passenger trade, since people were opting to travel to San Francisco or Los Angeles by Southern Pacific's new rails rather than by ship.

**The Pacific Coast Railway station in San Luis Obispo.**

A booming oil trade in Santa Maria prompted the Railway in 1909 to build an electric line to carry passengers from Santa Maria to Guadalupe where the Southern Pacific had its tracks. In 1911 it extended its line to an oil refinery at Palmer, a few miles southwest of Sisquoc. It turned out to be the last construction.

Automobiles were not yet common in 1912, a year when the Pacific Coast Railway carried a record-high 62,319 passengers, according to *Ships and Narrow Gauge Rails* by Gerald M. Best. A year later, however, buses proved formidable competition, and by 1922 passenger traffic had dropped to 3547 for the year. The electric line between Santa Maria and Guadalupe was finally discontinued in 1928.

Ironically, it was the same thing that eventually made the narrow-gauge train obsolete that gave the Pacific Coast Railway a brief revival. Gravel and crushed rock from a quarry near Sisquoc were the Railway's main freight during the late 1920s—freight that was used to build roads that soon took away most of the Railway's business.

In 1933, runs from Los Olivos to Los Alamos were discontinued, and the track was pulled up three years later. By 1941 the rest of the line was abandoned, and most of its engines, cars and track were sold for scrap or to narrow-gauge operations in other parts of the country.

Gordon Bennett, a native of Arroyo Grande, remembered the last days of the Pacific Coast Railway. In fact, he said with a laugh, he *should* have it on film.

"They tore out the rail when they went through downtown Arroyo Grande in 1942," he recalled. "I was down there taking movies of it. But there's nothing to see because my brother put the film in backwards."

Bennett recalled days as a boy when he and his friends made a "speeder" out of an apricot-drying cart, pushing it down the tracks (four people could ride it with two people pushing it, he said) on their way to school and scout meetings.

"We had a lot of fun with it," he said, "until the railway workers saw it sitting alongside the tracks and confiscated it."

He remembered the hobos who lived in cardboard shacks underneath the train bridge that spanned the creek in Arroyo Grande.

"We used to climb underneath the timbers on the bridge and smoke cigarettes," he said with a chuckle, "hoping that the train wouldn't come over and spill hot oil on us."

Bennett also recalled riding the train as it "rumbled down rickety old tracks" from Avila to Port Harford. "There was a lot of smoke and soot," he said. "It was kind of a dirty, oily, yucky deal." But he said this with fondness, adding that his parents and other old families in the area relied on the train to carry them to social functions and high school athletic events in Santa Maria and San Luis Obispo.

"It was their main source of transportation."

Like thousands of Americans, Bennett is an avid fan of trains. Another is Art Stump, who rode the Pacific Coast Railway on two of its very last trips, known as "Railfan Excursions." Stump remembered how, in 1937, he boarded the steam-powered Daylight Express in Los Angeles for a trip to Port Harford with several hundred other railroad enthusiasts.

"The ride was rather slow," he said. "They had a full train with lots of people and the track wasn't in that good a condition. I imagine it was 20 to 30 miles per hour at best."

It gave the passengers plenty of time to savor what Stump described as "nice little bridges and lovely scenery" on one of the last trips the train would make to Port Harford. The track was pulled up in 1942.

Stump in 1941 also boarded a Southern Pacific special train in Los Angeles, which again took him to San Luis Obispo, where he and a crowd of people rode the Pacific Coast Railway to Santa Maria and from there to Guadalupe, where the special train awaited to take the "railfans" back to Los Angeles.

*One of the Railway's two cabooses is restored and rests at the California State Railroad Museum in Sacramento*

"We all knew that it was going to be scrapped," explained Stump. "It was a nostalgia thing. And I thought, 'Well, this is my last chance to see the Pacific Coast Railway and ride on it.'"

Stump, Bennett and other railfans know where to find Pacific Coast Railway memorabilia. One of the cars, they said, has been restored and is on display at the Dallidet Adobe museum in San Luis Obispo. One of the Railway's two cabooses is also restored and rests at the California State Railroad Museum in Sacramento.

The other caboose, built in 1912, sits in the driveway of Railway fan Tom Petersen of Los Olivos. Petersen said he found the caboose about a year ago in nearby Buellton—just in time, he said, to save it from being "bulldozed and taken to the dump." Up to that point, the caboose had served as everything from rented living quarters to a playhouse for kids.

"There's a whole bunch of work that has to be done on it," he said. "It's close to a lifetime project, whether I want it or not! But to have half of the fleet of the Pacific Coast Railway's cabooses is a nice thing."

Stump even saw a bit of Pacific Coast Railway memorabilia in a place where he least expected it.

"I go almost every other year to a model engineer and train exhibit in London that has models from all over the world," he said. "A couple of years ago I was surprised to see a model of the Pacific Coast Railway at the exhibit. It was a pioneer railroad that grew up against a lot of odds."

*By January Anderson, December 1989*

T HE BLACK-AND-WHITE PHOTOGRAPH, its image slightly faded during the passing decades, is like thousands of surviving impressions of the Old West.

It was taken in 1886. A handful of anonymous people are shown clustered around a plain two-story frame building in the middle of nowhere. At the time, nowhere was the middle of northern Santa Barbara County. The building's name: the Central Hotel.

What distinguishes this photograph from its contemporaries is the fact that its subject survives—and thrives—more than a century later.

The Central Hotel soon became Mattei's Tavern. Some of the hotel's original rooms are now the dining rooms of a popular Los Olivos restaurant of the same name. The photograph hangs on one of the 100-year-old walls.

It is a testament to the pioneer Matteis—Felix and his wife Lucy. They created an elegant oasis in the wilderness, a familiar stopping point for road-weary travelers between San Francisco and Los Angeles and a popular resort for well-heeled Easterners.

The proprietor was born Falice Faustino Mattei in 1853 in Civio, Switzerland. He arrived in America at age 15 and rode the new transcontinental railroad to the West to work for relatives near San Francisco.

Working his way south, he married Lucy Fisher of San Luis Obispo in 1879. During the next seven years Mattei raised horses and dairy cattle, managed a hotel in Cayucos and a saloon in Los Alamos.

In 1886, Felix, Lucy and their three sons moved into a squatter's shack near a creek in present-day Los Olivos. Their neighbors were cattle ranchers, priests and Indian converts at Mission Santa Inez, and the folks operating a small stagecoach station in nearby Ballard.

That shack in the wilderness just happened to be the spot where barely a year later the narrow-gauge Pacific Coast Railway was to complete its line from San Luis Obispo. And the Railway was the only efficient link to the markets of

# The Matteis: Innkeepers in the Wilderness

**Felix Mattei, circa 1900, left, and Lucy Fisher Mattei**

Northern California.

The lone connection to the south was the stage over San Marcos Pass to Santa Barbara. Soon the stage office shifted from Ballard to Los Olivos; Mattei stood at the critical junction of stage and rail.

"A lot of people suggest that Felix was lucky as hell," said Jim Norris, editor of the Olive Press, a small publishing house in Los Olivos devoted to local history.

"But he was aware that this was going to be the end of the Pacific Coast Railway line," he said. "He knew all the people and was privy to what was happening. It was no fluke that he came to Los Olivos."

Mattei set up shop, serving food to the Railway construction crews while building his two-story, seven-room Central Hotel.

A competing hotel burned to the ground, giving Mattei a monopoly in the Santa Ynez Valley. Lucy's cooking gained a wide reputation among rail and stage passengers in California.

By the last decade of the century, word of Mattei's Tavern had spread far to the east. New arrivals were millionaires from New York and Chicago in search of a fashionable retreat in the West. The names Armour, Pillsbury and Vanderbilt are in the hotel registers.

*By the last decade of the century, word of Mattei's Tavern had spread far to the east*

"They came," said Norris, "to hunt bandtail pigeons, quail, duck, deer and geese. They'd do the hunting and Mattei's would prepare the food fresh."

Even when the Southern Pacific Railroad completed its north-south coastal link in 1901, bypassing Mattei's, business at the tavern continued to flourish.

The arrival of a Chinese cook, Gin Lung Gin, ushered in a 35-year era of elegant cuisine. Steelhead trout, abundant in the Santa Ynez River, were served free with every meal; elderberries for pies were picked from the river bottom; there were cattle, a cheese factory, fruit trees and a vegetable garden on Mattei's property.

Water for washing hair was drawn from an artesian well. One of few imports was drinking water shipped from Switzerland.

In almost every way it was a self-contained resort. "He had, in a sense, an empire going," Norris said. "There was a time when Mattei's had a reputation worldwide like Napa Valley has today."

In the background was Lucy, running the kitchen and raising a family of five sons.

"She looks stern (in photographs)," Norris said, "but apparently she didn't act that way. She was extremely hard working and extremely dedicated to the tavern."

But she was also a staunch supporter of the Women's Christian Temperance Union, and for a spell "they stopped serving liquor in the tavern."

Felix, who enjoyed an occasional sip of spirits, apparently sidestepped the prohibition.

**Mattei's Tavern at the height of its popularity.**
Photo/Santa Maria Valley Historical Society.

Said Ron Benson, a latter-day proprietor: "Bottles would be placed in cabinets and other hiding holes in the restaurant. When a drink was requested, it would be poured and the bottle whisked away so there would be no evidence."

Felix, according to Norris, was admired by all who knew him. He was extremely well-organized—at various times he managed Mattei's Tavern and three other area hotels.

He was an important figure in the Society of Los Alamos and the Rancheros Visitadores, private organizations that exist to this day.

When he died in 1930 (Lucy passed away in 1923), the funeral procession was three miles long, Norris said. "There were people in cars and others in buggies, a nice mixture of old and new."

A son, Fred, took over the management of the tavern for another colorful 25 years.

The present Stagecoach Room "was divided by a screen into a public office for Fred and a private poker and drinking room," said Benson. "Fred loved poker. People would go behind the screen and return lighter in cash but considerably refreshed."

The Mattei legacy ended with Fred's death in 1956, and ownership passed through several hands in succeeding years. A preservation group, Friends of Mattei's, purchased the tavern in 1973 and leased it to Chart House Restaurants.

Of course there have been changes over the century—a trellised porch was added along with additional dining rooms and a bar. The railroad siding and other buildings are long gone, and Mattei's has not received hotel guests for years.

The past is preserved in the old registers that greet restaurant guests and the memorabilia lining the old walls. There is a permanently locked door with "Stagecoach Office" painted on the glass above. It is the same door as the one pictured in that 105-year-old photo.

It is still Felix Mattei's place.

*By Bob Nelson, October 1986*

**A pioneer family arrives in Central City, California, soon to be renamed Santa Maria.**

# A Tale of Two Central Cities

I N 1874, THE Santa Maria Valley farming community known as Grangeville took a shiny new name: Central City.

A contemporary account suggests that a local businessman paid $50 for the honor of renaming the tiny settlement. He presumably chose the most grandiose title imaginable to lure traveling salesmen who would have to overnight in his hotel—the only one in town.

The innkeeper made one strategic error in the choice of the name. The local post office had been established years before as Santa Maria. Many letters and packages mailed to Central City, California—an address unrecognized by the U.S. Postal Department—simply vanished into a 19th century version of a bureaucratic Black Hole.

Something had to be done.

No problem, decided the town fathers—simply ask the federal government to change the name of the post office to Central City. They petitioned the Postal Department, fully expecting their reasonable request to be honored.

The answer came back quickly: a resounding *"NO!"*

Why not, they asked?

Because, explained the postal authorities with a withering blast of bureaucratic logic, there was already a Central City in Colorado, about 30 miles west of Denver. And sloppy handwriting could transform Central City, *Cal.*, into Central City, *Col.*, by a careless flick of the pen.

Maybe so. But it was almost impossible for any sane mailman to confuse the two. For while bibles and plow blades were being shipped into California's sedate Central

46

City, the Colorado version received crates of whiskey and cartons of bullets.

Central City, Colorado was a roaring mining camp clinging to the slope of a muddy hillside. Founded in 1859, the ramshackle town boomed and busted repeatedly as veins of gold were struck, then petered out. Brawling and shooting were a way of life in the saloon-infested, brothel-lined streets.

In 1874, the year when California's Central City was christened, much of the Colorado name-sharer burned down in a fire that started in a Chinese laborer's shanty. Frantic gold miners fought the conflagration with the only tools they had at hand—picks, shovels and dynamite. The cindered, demolished boomtown was quickly rebuilt. An ornate opera house rose from the ashes, constructed with four-foot thick stone walls as insurance against further disaster. It still stands today.

By 1882, when California's Central City was struggling to rename its post office, the Colorado version was in a miserable state of decline—the nearby ore deposits had finally been exhausted. Not much more than a ghost town, the Colorado community was stubbornly clinging to a spark of life.

But its post office had the name first.

So the inhabitants of the Santa Maria Valley, rebuffed by the federal postal authorities and sick of losing their mail, took the only reasonable course of action left to them. As an editorial in the *Santa Maria Times* sensibly pointed out: "If the post office name cannot be changed then the name of the town should be."

**Main Street in Central City, Colorado during its heyday.**

*Photos/Santa Maria Valley Historical Society and Colorado Historical Society*

47

In a citizens' meeting at Jones Music Hall on the evening of September 3, 1883, the name of Central City was abandoned. The town was officially rechristened Santa Maria to match the sign hanging on the local post office.

Over 100 years later, the two Central Cities are still about as different as any pair of communities can be.

Central City, Colorado, a National Historic Landmark, today numbers only about 350 permanent residents, far decreased from the thousands who called it home during its golden days. Gaudy saloons and gift shops draw a steady stream of tourists seeking an ersatz Old West. The sturdy opera house hosts summer performances by the New York Metropolitan and other leading opera and theater companies. A few of the ghost mines can still be inspected. And, thanks to a recent change in the state's liberal gambling laws, fledgling casinos have opened in the town, bringing a real estate boomlet of sorts.

In the meantime, Santa Maria has seen exploding growth from its 1882 population of 350 to over 55,000 today.

Other Central Cities have sprouted all over the map. Besides the one in Colorado, urban communities with that name are found in Arkansas, Iowa, Kentucky, Louisiana, Nebraska, Pennsylvania and South Dakota.

But thanks to the diligence of the U.S. Postal Service, no Central City exists in California.

*By Jon C. Picciuolo, August 1992*

T AMBO WAS a minstrel man—one of those old-time actors who blackened their faces with burnt cork, sang, danced, told stories, and otherwise cavorted in the long-forgotten minstrel shows that entertained 19th century American audiences.

More specifically, he was an end man. He sat at one end of a row of chairs on stage and, with his counterpart Bones at the other, fired wisecracks at the white-suited Mr. Interlocutor in the middle. He punctuated each sally with a rattle of his tambourine. Hence the name Tambo.

Tambo was down on his luck when he wandered into Santa Maria one December night in 1881. There was not much prospect for song-and-dance work, either, in the isolated ranching community of some 500 people.

Yet Tambo achieved a unique place in Santa Maria's history, a place he happily would have yielded to someone else.

He is the only man ever tarred, feathered and run out of the town on a rail.

Literally.

His real name was Michael Mullee, a cocky little Irishman who announced that he was also a good cook and soon proved it. He got a job cooking at one of the little boarding houses that fed many of the unmarried ranch workers. In a few months he saved enough money to start his own place on Main Street, which he grandly named the Delmonico Hotel after the glamorous and glittering New York society restaurant of the same name.

A small advertisement in the *Santa Maria Times* by M. Mullee, Proprietor, gives a hint of the airs he put on for his dingy establishment. Among the attractions he offered were:

• First-Class Family Accommodations at Prices to Suit

• Special Conveniences for Commercial Travelers—Large Sample Room

• Ladies' Private Oyster Saloon

• First Class Billiard Hall and Bar

Tambo quickly became the town clown. His brash manner, worldly air, and slightly risque tales of theatrical life piqued the interest of residents and visitors. When people were around, he was always "on," pulling stunts that called attention to himself.

One of his acts was to welcome guests to the Delmonico dining room with the bowing and scraping flourishes of a head waiter. He took the diners' orders, opened a sliding panel between dining room and kitchen, and called out the orders to the cook.

If time passed and Tambo was not to be seen, occasionally a diner would open the panel and peer into the kitchen. There he would find Tambo, encased in an apron, busily cooking the dinner at his wood-burning stove. A quick wave and wink from the proprietor-waiter-cook made the surprised guest feel that the two were sharing a cheerful secret.

After a few months, however, Tambo's act wore thin. He became a too-frequent patron of his own bar, and, when

# TAMBO: A STORY OF TAR AND FEATHERS

sufficiently stimulated, his cockiness became irritating.

Word got around that the name "hotel" was a euphemism for more unorthodox and intimate services, and that the offer of "Special Conveniences for Commercial Travelers" had a meaning beyond what the town's upright citizens anticipated.

The confines of the Delmonico saw drunken brawls, a slashing and a shooting. Finally, a self-appointed committee of righteous townsmen paid Tambo a visit.

"Get out of town within 48 hours" was their message.

For a generally quiet little community, Santa Maria had quite a strain of such vigilante activity. After all, the "law" was far away—over the mountains in Santa Barbara—and the town's lone constable knew when to step aside discreetly in the face of indignant citizens.

Two nights after the vigilantes gave Tambo his departure orders, they arranged a farewell party for him at the corner of Main and Broadway, the center of all the town's activity. The centerpiece was a cauldron of warm, oily tar heating over a bonfire.

Tambo arrived with the town constable at his side for protection. The vigilantes informed the constable that he was temporarily outside his jurisdiction, and the lawman quietly faded into the background.

"What are you going to do to me?" Tambo asked.

"Tar and feather you and run you out of the county on that rail." The spokesman pointed to a sawed-off tree limb from which the branches had been cut, leaving ugly little knobs.

To gather a crowd, the enforcers rang church bells and fired anvils. That is, they placed the bottoms of two anvils close together like pieces of bread in a sandwich, filled the gap with gunpowder, and exploded it with a long hot wire. The metallic BOOM resounded across the countryside.

Tambo tried to maintain his cocky air. Looking at the pole, he said, "That's all right, boys. Those knots will help me stick on." But his heart was not in it.

The vigilantes stripped Tambo in the October night chill, smeared him with tar, cut open a feather pillow and poured the fluffy white feathers over his body. He looked like a shivering white ghost.

When two of the men put the pole on their shoulders and told Tambo to straddle it, he refused. Someone ostentatiously twirled a rope, however, and he quickly accepted the invitation.

The bizarre torchlight procession headed north up the dirt road toward the Santa Maria River and the San Luis Obispo County line. The befeathered Tambo was shaking from the cold and humiliation.

But when the party passed the wagons of a traveling circus heading south from San Luis Obispo, Tambo's showman instincts surfaced and he played it for laughs.

"Do you want to buy an ostrich?" he shouted to the circus people.

*For a generally quiet little community, Santa Maria had quite a strain of vigilante activity*

# PUBLIC NOTICE

The undersigned are hereby notified to leave this town of Santa Maria on or before Sunday morning the 28th inst., at 9 o'clock, as you show no means of earning a legitimate livelihood. In event of not complying with the above you will be deal with accordingly.

## Joe Harp,
## E. Potter,
## Geo. Crawford,
## John Doe Drapper,
## Worth Brown,
## Dick Duke
## and Others.

By order of

## CITIZENS' COMMITTEE.

Santa Maria, Sept. 26th, 1884.

**The good citizens of Santa Maria let undesirables like Tambo know exactly where they stood.**

*Courtesy Santa Maria Valley Historical Society*

By then, the persecutors were losing interest in their game. They began to feel sorry for their victim. So they helped him wrestle his clothes on over the sticky tar and feathers and told him to walk the rest of the way to the river. At the river bank, they gave him his saddle horse, pointed north, and said, "Go!"

The old actor knew how to deliver an exit line. Mounting his horse, he said cheerfully, "Well, gentlemen, I hope next time we'll meet under more auspicious circumstances."

*By Phillip H. Ault, March 1990*

# THE BATTLE OF 'WHISKEY ROW'

**S**HANTY SALOONS were among the first structures built in Santa Maria, and almost from the beginning Santa Marians, both those who patronized them and those who abhorred them, called the lineup of bars on the north side of East Main Street near Broadway "Whiskey Row."

The name lingers with a nostalgic ring. The saloons have vanished, leaving a wide swath of lawn where glasses once clinked and poker chips rattled. Gone are the men who clustered at the mahogany bars, usually with their hats on, each with a foot on the brass rail. Gone is the pungent atmosphere reeking of stale beer and cigar smoke.

Gone, too, is the fright of little girls walking to the nearby Main Street School who, dutifully obeying their mothers' orders, crossed to the far side of the street when they approached Whiskey Row. Such terrible stories they had heard!

For more than 30 years, from the founding of Santa Maria in 1874 until the community finally voted to become a city in 1905, Whiskey Row was the center of a temperance battle.

Once, indeed, the power of the Row actually prevented Santa Maria from becoming incorporated.

Those who enjoyed Whiskey Row regarded it as something of a social club where a man could soothe his throat, brighten his spirits, eat a free lunch, argue farming and politics, and play poker for varied stakes. A prominent citizen once won a pair of colts in such a game. After discovering how much it cost to feed them, he found a game in another saloon where he intentionally lost the animals.

Those who sought to wipe out Whiskey Row as a community disgrace were led by the militant ladies of the Women's Christian Temperance Union (WCTU). Their group was so prominent that it even had a regular column in the weekly *Santa Maria Times*. The WCTU wives urged their men to make vigilante raids on the saloons when the occasional brawls got out of control.

Whiskey Row was a man's world, except for an occasional young woman of dubious credentials who may have slipped in a back door. No proper lady would be seen there.

Another staunch fighter against liquor in Santa Maria was one of the town's four founders, John Thornburg. Raised as a devout Quaker in Indiana, he vehemently opposed liquor. So when he placed 40 acres of his property at the southwest corner of Main and Broadway into the town plot, he included a deed restriction forbidding the sale of liquor on lots sold in his area.

Isaac Fesler, on whose northeast quadrant homestead property the Row stood, did not share Thornburg's passion for deed restrictions.

Neither the pleading of the WCTU nor the vigilante raids by self-appointed citizens committees had accomplished much. The sounds of whiskey-pouring continued to gurgle along the Row. When fire destroyed the block containing several saloons in 1884, cynics said with relish, "That fire did more to control Whiskey Row in a few minutes than the Citizens Committee has done in years."

Among the townspeople who volunteered to carry goods from the threatened and burning buildings were several WCTU members. As they dashed into the saloons, the women faced a dilemma. Should they do their civic duty and save property, or should they destroy the tools of the enemy? The editor of the *Times* commented wryly that only a few of the ladies were seen smashing bottles.

Whiskey Row was quickly rebuilt.

In 1895 civic leaders decided that the time had come to incorporate Santa Maria as a city. The "drys" promoted incorporation as a way to control the saloons, which then would be under municipal rather than county supervision. The "wets" opposed incorporation strenuously. They liked things just as they were, since county government far away in Santa Barbara virtually ignored the saloons.

Leaders of the wet forces were far too shrewd to campaign on a "let's-keep-the-saloons" platform. Instead, they concentrated on scaring voters with claims that their taxes would go up under incorporation. In handbills scattered around town, they raised bogeymen that caused shivers in the pocketbook. Residents were warned that they would have to pay to install sidewalks outside their homes and to have the city's dirt streets sprinkled, among other extravagances of a spendthrift city council.

The pro-incorporation forces climbed onto the high moral ground. One said in a letter to the *Times:* "If this moral question is of no importance, then we had as well close up our schools and churches, and let the evil influences have their way ... it is impossible to get better class people to settle here when they see so many vicious places open, and no incorporation to even regulate them."

Santa Maria voters faced that ancient conflict, money vs. morals. As so often happens, money won, and incorporation was defeated 100-90.

The vote seems very small for such an angry election. But there were reasons. The official election notice stated that the population within the proposed city boundaries was 750. Women were still a quarter century away from having the right to vote. Neither could the children, of course, and families were large in those days.

The frustrated members of the WCTU complained, "If only we had been allowed to vote! Things would have been different." Probably they would have been.

The *Times* editor commented, "The people said by their votes, better suffer the evils we know than the evils we know not."

Another 10 years passed before cityhood boosters dared to put incorporation to an election test again, on Sept. 12, 1905.

The community had grown a bit, and the mood had changed. Sensing that they would lose, the saloon faction late

*Santa Maria voters faced that ancient conflict, money vs. morals*

In the 1930s saloons on Whiskey Row were polished and clean. But three decades earlier they were less appealing and the target of temperance activists.
*Photo/Santa Maria Valley Historical Society*

on election day tried to sneak in a number of unregistered voters from the oil fields to cast ballots. Tense confrontations took place as the election judges rejected the "ringers."

Incorporation was approved by 63 votes, 202-139.

The newly created city council wasted no time. At its first meeting it adopted City Ordinance No. 1, imposing a municipal license tax on places selling liquor. Saloons were taxed $75 every three months, limited to 10 in number, and made subject to losing their licenses if the council found they were conducted in a disorderly manner or were public nuisances.

The temperance forces had won, at last. But despite their owners' fears, the saloons survived. Whiskey Row remained a Santa Maria institution for another 50 years, albeit considerably subdued. It enjoyed boom times during the wars, grimly shut down during the years of national Prohibition, then joyously reopened after Repeal in 1933. By the early 1950s, however, it was a shabby ghost of the old days.

The entire line of saloons and other buildings in the block was torn down in 1959 to make way for the present Central Plaza.

On the site of Whiskey Row, surrounded by lawn, stands a fountain that clearly is *not* a memorial to the saloons, because it pours out only water.

*By Phillip H. Ault, June 1990*

ITEM FROM the *Santa Maria Times*, April 25, 1930: "Dr. W.T. Lucas was taken to the Santa Maria Hospital yesterday evening at 6 o'clock following a collision with an unknown motorist in the 200 block of South Vine Street. Other than several cuts and bruises the pioneer physician was found to be unhurt this morning and was discharged after receiving treatment. The machine which Lucas was driving was not badly damaged, although one front wheel was torn away and the fenders smashed in."

Apparently, Dr. William Thomas Lucas never did get the hang of an automobile. He was better suited to the horse and buggy, the vehicle he had driven into the Santa Maria Valley a half century earlier.

"He'd drive up to our door, pull up his horse, fling the lines to anyone who happened to be handy, jump out of his buggy and come stamping into the house," one resident recalled years earlier.

"'How'n hell's that patient?' he'd boom, and somehow you'd just know diseases didn't have a chance with him around."

Remember "Doc" from the television series *Gunsmoke?* His gruff, gnarled exterior hid a deep devotion to the practice of medicine and the people of a frontier town.

Add a few pounds and a bushy mustache, and the Doc image mirrors the real-life Dr. Lucas of Santa Maria.

By all accounts, the doctor was not averse to using profanity or consuming alcohol. And records show that he never let it interfere with what became a 24-hour-a-day business of doctoring from Cuyama to Los Alamos.

Anecdotes from Lucas' 50-plus years in Santa Maria could fill volumes. Many tales revolve around his misadventures with the motorcar.

"He was good at horses," recalled Ted Bianchi, who was a Lucas patient as a youth, "but when it came to driving an automobile, he was pretty clumsy."

Winston Wickenden recalled a story of Lucas hastening in his Model T to Santa Maria Hospital, a converted rooming house on South Broadway.

"As he went by the hospital people saw him holding the steering wheel and yelling 'Whoa!'" Wickenden said.

"He came walking back later. When he was asked what had happened, he said he'd tried to make a U-turn while going full bore and had tipped over.

"He just left the car laying there on its side in the middle of Broadway, and he came running to the hospital with his black bag."

Others say that both ends of the doctor's garage were open so he could drive in one end and out the other.

Townspeople forgave Lucas' inability to master a new technology of the 20th century. By that time he was 80 years old and had seen much change.

Born in Missouri in 1850, Lucas traveled as a youth by wagon train to Montana and later to Northern California. He

# THE DOCTOR MADE HOUSE CALLS IN HIS CARRIAGE

In his later years, Dr. W.T. Lucas was a beloved member of the community ... as long as he wasn't driving.

*Photo/Santa Maria Valley Historical Society*

worked his way through medical school and in 1879 arrived in the bustling farm town of Guadalupe.

Nearby Central City—soon to be renamed Santa Maria—slowly overtook Guadalupe as the population center of the valley, and Lucas followed his patients to Santa Maria.

Much later, Lucas told a writer that he was the first licensed physician in the area.

"There was an M.D., or perhaps several, in Santa Barbara, and others in San Luis Obispo," he said. "There is a stretch of 110 miles in between, and I took care of the people in it, although there were some old fellows, unlicensed, who used to do a little volunteer healing."

His black bag contained many of the period's most modern instruments and remedies. (Some articles are on display at the Santa Maria Valley Historical Society Museum.)

However, Lucas had his own brand of pioneer doctoring. He told his patients that good health involved only two factors—circulation and elimination.

Surgery was a last resort. When young Wickenden badly injured his hand in a freak shooting accident, Lucas considered amputation. But he decided to wait overnight; circulation returned to the injured hand and it was saved.

Appendicitis was Wickenden's woe a few years later.

"Now they would take the appendix right out," Wickenden said. "But he (Lucas) didn't buy that. He put ice packs on it for five days and I came out of it."

Decades later, Wickenden was X-rayed for another illness and doctors were unable to locate his appendix on the film. "Those ice packs had dried it up completely, I think," he said. "It has never bothered me since."

Fees? Lucas often accepted farm produce in lieu of cash. Sometimes the ledger entries of some patients read "Paid by God" when death closed an account.

If his accounting methods were different, so was his use of language. A dose of profanity was sometimes part of the cure.

Bianchi remembered coming down ill and being bundled up in a turtleneck sweater by his mother. "Dr Lucas came in our house," he said, "and in a gruff voice he asked me, 'Where the hell are you going—a prize fight' With that turtleneck sweater I looked like the prizefighters of that day."

Another Lucas patient, Raymond Sharp Stearns, once remarked, "Doc was known to say a whole sentence at a time without a cuss word—but that didn't happen often."

Lucas was also known to use alcohol as more than a temporary painkiller. Most mornings he could be seen lumbering from his office near the intersection of Pine and Chapel streets to a favored bar on "Whiskey Row," a storied stretch of saloons, diners, card rooms and markets on Main Street east of Broadway.

"They would make him sort of a toddy—milk, an egg and a shot of whiskey," Wickenden said. "They would shake it all up, and that is how he started his day.

"But he never drank on the job," he added. "He took his work seriously."

His vices were generally dismissed, and Lucas was a frequent master of ceremonies at official functions. His booming voice and heavyset figure, clothed in shades of gray and with a gold watch chain spanning his vest, lent an air of authority to the laying of cornerstones in the growing community.

And he labored long and hard at medicine. He treated dozens of victims soon after the calamitous San Francisco earthquake in 1906. He helped establish the first hospital between Santa Barbara and San Luis Obispo in 1906 (the room rate at Santa Maria Hospital was $4 a day!).

His impact was such that during a lodge meeting Lucas was able to pick out 32 men whom he had brought into the world.

By the time he succumbed to pneumonia in 1931, the pioneer doctor had left every patient with a priceless story.

For instance, at an American Medical Association meeting in San Francisco, Lucas and other doctors were caught up in a meandering discussion of kissing. In that Victorian period, some thought of kissing as dangerous and unsanitary and maintained that the practice should be abolished.

The doctor from Santa Maria stood and put the subject to rest, saying, "Gentlemen, I move that this body go on record as recommending that kissing be banned ... unless administered by a physician."

Of such utterances are legends made.

*By Bob Nelson, October 1984*

*'Doc was known to say a whole sentence at a time without a cuss word—but that didn't happen often'*

# A GOLD RUSH IN LOMPOC

I N FEBRUARY 1889, a mysterious stranger arrived in the Lompoc Valley. Neither farmer nor merchant, he kept to himself and quietly began to dig near the mouth of the Santa Ynez River.

The *Lompoc Record* editor, smelling a story, hitched up his buggy and drove out to the beach to see what was going on.

His newspaperman's nose had not lied.

*Gold!!* announced the stranger, a veteran prospector who had trekked to the valley to investigate old rumors of riches in the sands. There was, he swore, enough gold hidden in the beach to keep a thousand miners busy for years—plenty for all! As proof, he sent the editor back to town with a jar of the precious stuff to display in the general store.

Word spread quickly. The yellow metal, powder-fine and known as "flour gold," nestled in scattered layers of black sand near the Santa Ynez estuary.

In only a few weeks, several pounds of golden treasure were extracted and sold in San Francisco.

Lompoc's stunned townsfolk swung into action. Within a month the first mining company had formed, placing orders for tools and machinery. Right on its heels the boundaries of a mining district, covering the coast from the river's mouth southward to Honda Creek, were staked and filed with the county. Individual mining claims were limited to 1500 feet along the surf line; one day's work in every 30 was sufficient to hold a claim.

Lompoc's gold rush was on!

By June 1889, several mining teams were scrabbling away. Typically, five miners manned a large wooden "rocker" into which they shovelled gold-bearing sand. They shook the contraption back and forth vigorously as buckets of sea water washed away the sand, leaving the heavier grains of gold clinging to woolen blanket strips nailed along the rocker's bottom. Each team recovered around $30 of metal a day, a little more than an ounce.

When the tide rolled in, the heavy rockers were dragged up the beach to dry ground; when the water receded, back they went. The miners combed the same black sand over and over. Amazingly, the sea seemed to replenish the precious metal as fast as men could pull it out! On one glorious day in late June, 12 ounces of gleaming dust were extracted by a single mining company.

It was cold, miserable labor—the tough miners worked barefoot in the chilly surf. High waves pounded the men and their gear. Not very many men got rich. Most of the profits went to the claim holders, while each contract miner earned about $2 a day plus food and a rough canvas cot under a tent. Some claim bosses, greedy for fatter profits, hired Chinese laborers who worked for $1 a day and no board.

By December 1889, every claim on the coast was occupied. A small army of 200 miners battled howling winds and roaring surf to snatch treasure from the sand.

More efficient methods were devised to pry out the riches. Often hundreds of tons of worthless beach were scraped away to uncover the coveted black layers. Every now and then a lucky storm helped the miners, rolling in from the Pacific to scour the beach and expose the prize.

Wagon loads of ore sand were collected at low tide, hauled above the high water mark and dumped into enormous sluice boxes. Horse-driven water pumps flushed the gold-bearing loads through the sluices. Quicksilver slathered onto copper plates captured the precious particles before they swept away.

Daily wages soared to $5 per man. The frantic pace continued into early 1890 as costly ore separators, each capable of processing 50 tons per day, were shipped into the Lompoc Valley. One lucky claim boss netted a profit of over $1200 in less than a month. Articles about Lompoc's bonanza ran in New York and Los Angeles newspapers.

But Mother Nature can be maddeningly fickle with her gifts, the Lompoc miners soon learned.

Throughout the spring and summer of 1890, yields steadily declined. The gold slowly petered out. Claims were abandoned as the cost of extracting gold exceeded the value of the metal—toward the end it cost $10 to mine a dollar's worth. Dismayed investors watched their idle, expensive machinery transformed into rusty junk.

The ocean, which had once been an ally, became an enemy, reburying the magic layers of black sand under many feet of worthless cover.

Daily wages fell to $1.50; many miners drifted away to easier jobs. Soon only a few stubborn souls remained, glumly panning the played-out sands for enough gold to cover their food bills.

As late as 1930, sporadic attempts were made to reopen the diggings. For a while it seemed that gasoline engines could bring about a technological miracle, cheaply pumping high volumes of sand and water onshore faster than the sea could snatch it back. But once again the mighty Pacific won, wrecking all the machinery that was installed near the surf.

Lompoc's beach mines are long gone, but one question still remains unanswered.

Whence came all the gold?

The old Lompoc miners cherished a favorite theory: Somewhere offshore a rich ledge of gold—a true Mother Lode—protrudes from the sea bottom. Grinding sands and swift ocean currents are slowly eroding the metal. If true, then perhaps in a few centuries another golden treasure will be ripe for harvesting from the sands of the Central Coast.

*By Jon C. Picciuolo, March 1993*

**A steam shovel loads an ore cart with gold-bearing sand from the beach near Lompoc.**
*Photo/Lompoc Valley Historical Society*

# SECTION II

## GROWING UP
## 1900-1939

# The Great Quake of 1902

**J**ULY OF 1902 brought a long spell of still, sultry days to the Central Coast. Old-timers swore it was perfect earthquake weather, earning the usual chorus of snickers from their neighbors.

In Los Alamos, the doubters quickly became believers.

Distant rumblings, felt beneath the little town for several weeks, had been mostly ignored. Then on Sunday, July 27, shortly before 11 p.m., a violent shock brought the townsfolk reeling from their beds. The sharp jolt was felt as far away as Santa Barbara.

Bone-dry Los Alamos Creek became a rushing torrent, 18 feet wide by two deep, as local aquifers were tortured and squeezed. Jagged cracks ripped through the thick earthen walls of adobe dwellings.

At the nearby Western Union Oil Company field, in production for only a year, crude oil tanks were tossed around like flimsy toys. More than 3000 barrels of reeking petroleum sloshed out of the ruptured steel plating and shattered pipes.

But aside from frayed nerves, frightened livestock, and a few broken chimneys, very little harm was done in the town.

The worst was yet to come.

For the next several days Los Alamos was racked by a series of ever-intensifying temblors felt all over Santa Barbara County. Panicked residents leapt outdoors whenever the ground began to move. They set up housekeeping in the streets and vacant lots, cooking and sleeping in the open to escape falling plaster and toppling furniture. They were there, huddled around campfires waiting for the dawn, when the monster quake hit at 1:20 a.m. on Thursday, July 31.

Starting with a rumble like distant thunder and building to the roar of "a thousand cannon," the violent earthquake thrashed a slice of the Central Coast 15 miles long by four wide. Gaping fissures tore through canyons and open fields. Springs of water spurted where none had existed before.

Terrified Los Alamos citizens clung to each other in the dark and prayed while their town disintegrated around them.

The Catholic chapel crumbled into pieces of kindling. The Presbyterian church's roof crashed down, its bell tower toppled. Historic old adobes, battered but still standing after the earlier quakes, collapsed into dusty ruins. Water tanks keeled over, their latticework supports buckling like the legs of a drunk.

Brick walls crumpled and folded. Not a chimney remained standing; not one pane of glass was unsmashed. Redwood-framed homes and stores, lightly-built and flexible, survived relatively intact, but their contents were reduced to jumbled piles of trash. Many Los Alamos buildings bounced off their foundations.

In the dismal aftermath, no solace could be bought at the local saloon owned by the town's justice of the peace—each bottle and glass had been destroyed. Every jar of medicine was shattered in the town's only drugstore. One or two fires broke out but were quickly extinguished.

The vicious earthquake was described by many as a "twister"—the ground heaved and plunged while it swayed in a circular, sickening motion. The disturbance, felt as far south as Los Angeles and as far north as San Luis Obispo, caused minor damage in Lompoc where walls of the Hotel Arthur cracked and split. The Santa Ynez River, driven underground in the midsummer heat, briefly bubbled to the surface. Landslides blocked the Harris Grade between Los Alamos and the Lompoc Valley. Pendulum clocks stopped in Guadalupe. Santa Maria and Santa Barbara were strongly shaken.

Miraculously, no one was killed or seriously injured, but the weary Los Alamos population had endured enough. Civic leaders begged the University of California at Berkeley for advice. The university's telephoned reply was instantaneous and unmistakable: evacuate your town, flee for your life!

Teams were harnessed and family after family moved out along the country roads. Some headed for Santa Maria and San Luis Obispo, others for Lompoc or Santa Barbara. After hasty track repairs, a special 14-car train of the now-defunct Pacific Coast Railway, a narrow-gauge line, hauled evacuees northward from Los Alamos to safety. A few men remained behind to stand guard over the wreckage and watch for fires.

Newspapers were quick to report the exciting story, garbling facts with wild rumors. One Los Angeles paper reported that the City of Santa Barbara had sustained terrible damage accompanied by weird rainbows ringing the sun and other strange celestial phenomena. Santa Barbara's press, fearing a loss of business and tourism, issued immediate denials. Lompoc's newspaper took similar action.

A San Francisco editor breathlessly reported the eruption of a huge volcano near Los Alamos. This fantastic claim brought much-needed laughter to the Central Coast, even as aftershocks rocked the area. Another Bay Area newspaper congratulated its readers for being so far away from Santa

San Francisco readers learned of the destructive power of an earthquake years before their own disaster.

Barbara during the earthquake season.

Experts-for-pay filled columns of print with unproven notions of what had triggered the earthquakes. Shifting, churning deposits of oil and natural gas was a favorite theory.

The July 31 temblor was widely heralded as one of the state's worst ever. One Chicago paper, trying to hold things in perspective, pointed out that all the known California earthquakes put together could not equal the destructiveness of the infamous 1886 South Carolina jolt—remember, the Los Alamos quake was about four years before the 1906 San Francisco horror.

In an effort to profit from the tremors, a Santa Barbara hardware store advertised sturdy hammocks for sale—strong enough for two and guaranteed to give undisturbed sleep through earthquakes.

Aftershocks continued through December 1902 before finally subsiding to a solitary jolt every now and then. Townsfolk drifted back to Los Alamos and resumed their lives.

A handful of buildings from that time can still be seen in the little town, including the general store, the Presbyterian church and the old railroad depot—plucky survivors of the great 1902 earthquake.

*By Jon C. Picciuolo, September 1993*

The stunning La Grande Pavilion attracted a large crowd for its opening in 1905.

AMERICANS HAVE A right to gloat at the triumph of capitalism over communism. But they should not forget to tell all those former communists longing to be free enterprisers that the U.S. system has created its fair share of messes.

Fledgling capitalists should know that an economy founded on a free people's willingness to take risks and an unwillingness to accept failure continues to provide myriad goods and services for many and vast riches for some.

However, they also should know that this go-for-broke attitude is sometimes accompanied by poor planning and management, sending untold billions "down a rat hole."

Frequently that misspent money creates something beautiful, a monument to the occasional folly of free enterprise. Sadly, succeeding generations rarely see these creations. Since they fail to turn a profit, they are allowed to crumble and vanish.

Such was the case with La Grande Pavilion, a remarkable turn-of-the-century structure built in the dunes near Oceano. It was ballyhooed across America as the elegant centerpiece of a budding seaside community.

But within a few years of its opening La Grande Pavilion stood empty, isolated and forgotten, a target for destruction by vandals and the elements.

At the dawn of the 20th century, a beach town revolving around a stunning pavilion seemed like a winning proposition to speculators like the managers of the Golden State Realty Company of Los Angeles.

For years the benign climate of the Pismo Beach area had been a magnet for residents of the overheated San Joaquin Valley. Families in Fresno and Bakersfield would pack up a wagon and spend the summer at the dunes.

# THE LOST PAVILION

When the Southern Pacific Railroad arrived in Pismo Beach, real estate promoters were not far behind. Golden State Realty chose a spot for its colony near Oso Flaco Lake, about two miles south of present-day Oceano.

La Grande Pavilion rose in 1905—a grand example of the Victorian architecture of the day. Two stories high, it was dominated by three church-like towers. The second level was an elegantly appointed dance floor complete with hardwood floor and double-pane glass. The first floor was partitioned into offices for the swarming real estate agents; later it was to be converted to shops, boutiques and other small businesses.

A large water tank was built nearby to serve the pavilion and the settlers to come. Power lines were run to each building and a 700-foot pier was built on the beach a few yards away. Plans were drawn for landscaped grounds and cement sidewalks.

The real estate promoters subdivided the land around La Grande Pavilion into thousands of lots—prices starting at $50. Prospective colonists arrived by train from Los Angeles and San Francisco. Readers across the nation heard of the good life on the Central Coast.

"They advertised heavily on the East Coast and they sold a lot of property," said Arroyo Grande businessman Gordon Bennett, who researched the history of San Luis Obispo County. "It was a common thing back in those days. There weren't so many rules and regulations."

The pavilion and subdivision opened with a celebration of music and dance as hundreds of people arrived in their horse-drawn buggies via the beach or on a gravel road leading from nearby Oceano. Many were landowners viewing for the first time the property they had purchased by mail.

Soon after the impressive opening, though, painful reality set in. The colonists discovered that they had purchased piles of shifting sand; marking their property—let alone building on it—was almost impossible.

Blowing sand soon obliterated the gravel road, and the pier washed away in rough seas. "There was no access, only from the beach," Bennett said. "At high tide it was hard to get in. The people who bought ... saw that it was hopeless. Nobody would live there."

While the promoters of La Grande Pavilion realized their shortsightedness and slowly abandoned the project ("They took a gamble," Bennett says, "but it didn't come through"), other entrepreneurs in nearby Pismo Beach were moving forward with a better-conceived idea.

Capitalizing on its reputation as a resort area, Pismo Beach promoters in 1907 built a pavilion joining two hotels, a bathhouse and amusement park. Tourists flocked to the area and stayed in a large tent city on the beach. Known in later years as a dance hall featuring the top Big Band orchestras, the pavilion burned to the ground in the 1940s.

That was long after the site of La Grande Pavilion became "like a Nevada ghost town," said Harold Guiton, a Realtor

*The real estate promoters subdivided the land around La Grande Pavilion into thousands of lots—prices starting at $50*

The Pavilion's church-like towers were a splendid example of Victorian-era architecture.

*Courtesy Bennett-Loomis archives, Virgil Hodges photos*

and history buff in Oceano.

Vandals smashed the windows and tore up the hardwood floor. "There was a grand piano in the balcony," Guiton recalled. "The vandals pushed it over the edge and it crashed right through the floor."

Nature performed its own vandalism.

"Sand had blown under one corner of the building and you could walk right under it," Guiton recalled. "It was ready to collapse."

Collapse it did a few years later when Guiton's father bought the building for salvage. What the wrecking crew left behind, The Dunites—a group of free spirits who populated the dunes in the 1930s—used to build their ramshackle dwellings.

The shifting dunes covered all traces of La Grande Pavilion. Winter storms and passing dune buggies occasionally reveal a weather-beaten piece of siding, shards of glass, electrical wire or plumbing.

For Norm Hammond, a San Luis Obispo firefighter and chronicler of life in the dunes, the lost pavilion evoked a sad memory from 1973.

"We were having a training exercise," he recalled, "and I was waiting to touch off a fire in a rundown auto court when I found out it had been built with lumber from La Grande Pavilion.

"What could I do? I would have liked to have saved some of it, but everything was ready (for the training fire), and I had to go through with it."

A sad ending, indeed, for a work of art cast aside by free enterprise.

*By Bob Nelson, November 1985*

# 'OLD MAUD': BIRTH OF AN OIL BOOM

DRILLING FOR OIL is a numbers game—a dirty, sweaty, dangerous game of chance. Year after year oilmen throw the dice, ignoring one losing roll after another while anticipating that multi-million-dollar bonanza.

Geologists map out likely sources of oil and hard-bitten drilling crews poke one hole after another into the earth. Most holes are "dusters" that yield nothing; an active well may produce only a few barrels a day.

Every oil well, producer or dry hole, is designated in the company records by field and number, such as Pinal No. 5 or Adams No. 3. Thousands of wells—bringing forth the life-blood of an industrial society—receive no more recognition than a few pen strokes in a ledger book. After all, they are merely holes in the ground.

But occasionally one hole in the ground becomes special, endearing, with its own personality. Then the drilling crews dignify it with a nickname.

Such was the case with Hartnell No. 1, which a Union Oil Company crew spudded in the rolling hills on the southern edge of the Santa Maria Valley in 1904. The workers dubbed it "Old Maud."

They had good reason. Old Maud turned out to be a gusher, one of the all-time greats. In its heyday, Old Maud was the biggest producing oil well in history and helped turn the fledgling oil industry from a hit-and-miss proposition into the prime source of energy in the 20th century.

And it was a lucky mistake. If the workers had followed directions and drilled the hole where it was supposed to be drilled, Old Maud might have been just another number in the company records.

Old Maud was not the first oil well drilled in northern Santa Barbara County. Exploration began in the late 1800s, and by the end of 1903 the region had 22 wells producing about 8,000 barrels a day.

The good fortune was primarily the result of the work of W.W. Orcutt, a young Union Oil Company geologist. He began mapping the area in 1901 and recommended that the company purchase leases for 70,000 acres in the vicinity of the present-day community that bears his name.

Orcutt designated several spots as drilling sites with great potential. One spot was on property owned by the Hartnell family. However, a crew mistakenly constructed its derrick about 65 feet from the spot where Orcutt said to drill.

"Back in those days, 1904, nobody thought a few feet one way or the other made much difference," recalled Jack Reed, a member of the crew, in the book The 76 Bonanza. "It was a hot day, and when the boiler accidentally fell off the wagon where the derrick would have been, we left it right there and put up the derrick where the enginehouse should have been.

"The boss was mad, but not quite mad enough to make us tear down a whole day's work and start over again."

They spudded in June 22, and on December 2 the ground

began to rumble. "Then with a roar," Reed said, "a column of oil and gas shoots up through the rig floor to a height of 150 feet. Oil begins to pour down the gullies and creek beds."

It was the birth of a gusher that would discharge a million barrels in its first 100 days. It could not be capped; when someone mistakenly closed the valve on the well, oil began spouting from every squirrel and gopher hole within 100 yards.

"The surrounding fields are full of miniature geysers of oil," said Reed.

To prevent the oil from rushing uncontrolled into nearby

**The historic Old Maud well at the height of her glory.**

watershed, the crews trapped the flow with a series of earthen dams, said Darwin Sainz of Los Alamos, a Unocal engineer who studied oil development in the region.

"They built dikes and berms," he said, "and when one would overflow it would begin to fill another one. It went on like that right down the hill.

"Eventually a shipyard in San Francisco built tank cars just for this well, and they pumped the oil in and hauled it out."

What caused a gusher of such magnitude? The good fortune to strike at just the right spot, said Sainz.

"Most people think that oil is just sitting in the ground in a pool," he explained. "But oil and natural gas have a way of migrating to certain pockets ... geological formations, and not all of the formations have oil.

"They probably hit right on top of the structure, and the gas came first and then all the oil ... like poking a hole in a balloon."

The crew originally nicknamed their historic well "The Kaiser" after the German leader who was making quite a bit of international noise at the time. But after a few months the moniker "Old Maud" stuck.

The origin of the name is uncertain. One story claims Old Maud was a driller's mule; another that it honored someone's mother; yet another that it was a tribute to a local prostitute.

What is clear is the impact Old Maud and its abundance of quality crude had on the oil business.

"It put the industry on the map," said Sainz. "Oil stocks went crazy, and lot of big money began to be spent.

"It was the first time that people didn't pooh-pooh the oil industry. Before (Old Maud) they didn't think there was enough oil in the ground. Now the big-money backers saw that it had a future."

Old Maud's future was awe inspiring. Averaging at its peak almost 12,000 barrels a day, it flowed for two years and yielded nearly 3 million barrels before it was finally put on a pump.

Pumping continued for 12 years. In 1918, while still producing 250 barrels a day, Old Maud's eight-inch casing collapsed. Company officials decided that refitting the well would be too expensive, and the hole was closed.

But in 1943 wartime demand for oil made it feasible to resurrect shut-in wells. Old Maud was cleaned out, a new pump installed, and the well yielded 175 barrels a day to once again become one of the field's top producers.

By then the Santa Maria Valley was reaching its peak as an oil-producing region. During the 1940s the valley had as many as 45 rigs yielding up to 45,000 barrels a day.

In 1955 Old Maud was closed again, this time for good, with a tally of 5 million barrels beside its name in company records. The site of the well—about 1-1/4 miles east of Highway 1 and south of Orcutt—was reclaimed by nature; cattle graze in the fields that once held pools of oil.

*'Eventually a shipyard in San Francisco built tank cars just for this well'*

And there is a kicker to this story. Union Oil drilled a sister well next to its landmark gusher, in the exact spot where Old Maud was supposed to go.

It produced only 65 barrels on its best day.

*By Bob Nelson, October 1985*

**Note: Much of the material in this article is contained in the book *Old Town Orcutt: A Small California Oil Town Remembered*, published in 1987 by the Orcutt Historical Committee. It is available at the Santa Maria Valley Historical Museum and other Central Coast bookstores.**

**Newfound affluence for these oil investors is reflected in one of the pools of crude at the Old Maud drilling site.**

*Photos/Santa Maria Valley Historical Society*

# THE COWBOYS: 30 BUCKS A MONTH AND NO COMPLAINTS

**H**ISTORY BOOKS say the golden age of the cowboy ended in the mid-1880s.

Maybe. By that time the West's wide-open spaces were practically fenced in, and the huge herds of cattle of the 1870s were thinned by poor weather, bad range management and a dramatic drop in prices. After less than a generation, the idealized image of the cowboy—freewheeling, stoic, living and dying by the Code of the West—was disappearing.

However, America retained its appetite for beef. Through the next century cattlemen met that demand, and cowboys were their point men on the range.

The cowboys began riding in pickup trucks rather than on horses. And often they were asked to plow a hayfield—once dismissed as a job for "sodbusters"—as well as perform the normal cowboy chores of repairing fences and doctoring cattle.

But they still wore the same garb, threw the same lariats and battled the same elements as their predecessors.

The Wilson brothers—Raymond "Dutch" and Lawrence "Link"—were cowboys on the Central Coast beginning in the 1920s. They worked Fred Bixby's Cojo Ranch as well as the Jalama, San Marcos and Los Alamos.

They arose at 4 a.m., worked often to dusk and lived in a bunkhouse heated only by a wood stove, their belongings usually stuffed into a suitcase and slid under the bed. They killed time in the evening playing cards in the light of a coal oil lamp.

The pay for most cowboys was $40-45 a month plus board, although wages dropped to $30 during the Depression of the 1930s. "We didn't kick," said Link. "We didn't know any better, and they fed us good."

Dutch, 77, and Link, 80, talked about their five decades in the business over a bowl of beef jerky in Dutch's Santa Ynez home ...

## COWBOY GEAR

Most cowboys agreed with Bixby that the wide-brimmed, 10-gallon-style hats popular elsewhere in the Southwest simply would not do on the Central Coast. "You couldn't keep them on," said Dutch. "On those ranches the wind blew 360 days a year."

The Wilsons preferred a Stetson with a 3 to 3-1/2-inch brim and low crown. "It was for protection," said Link, "but it was a custom, too."

A colorful bandanna was another customary part of the cowboy outfit; on the ranch it insulated against the cold morning fog or hot afternoon sun. It was sometimes used as a tourniquet in case of a cut or snakebite.

And, Dutch recalled, "when you were following cattle on the real dusty roads you'd pull it over your nose and it was much easier to breathe."

Most riders wore wide leather "batwing" chaps—pronounced "shaps"—that could be fastened in the back without removing boots and spurs. They helped the cowboy grip the saddle better and offered protection against rain, chafing and prickly patches of dry brush.

"In cactus country they were a must," said Dutch.

The true cowboy wore boots with a reinforced arch and higher heel to fit into the stirrups. Spurs were usually simple, with a star-shaped rowel used to prod the cowboy's mount. "Most guys hardly ever took them off," said Dutch. "That way you knew where they were and wouldn't forget them."

### RIDING

Riding, or the lack of it, is the biggest difference between the ranch horses in the 1920s and 30s—Appaloosas, thoroughbreds and palominos—and the more-pampered modern mounts, the brothers said.

"Now you have a much better type and quality of horse ... much better breeding," said Dutch. "But they don't get as much work. They're not as well broke.

"In the old days you would take three or four rides every day to check things at the ranch. Now they put the horse in a

trailer and ride out with a pickup or 4-wheel drive to the area they want to check."

All the professional training in the world cannot substitute for months of day-to-day work on a ranch, they claimed. "We took three years to finish a horse in the old days," said Dutch. "Now they do it in three to six months."

Breaking was in the time-honored cowboy tradition. First the young horse was introduced to a halter and led around the main corral to become accustomed to the metal in its mouth. Next the cowboy rode the horse in a small corral.

**Cowboys guard a herd at the turn of the century.**
*Photo/Santa Maria Valley Historical Society*

Then it was out into the hills.

"You had to get a little respect so (the horse) wouldn't take advantage of you," said Dutch. "You didn't want it to think you were afraid of it."

Some horses bucked every time they were mounted, Link said. Others liked to surprise their riders.

"The first time it might not buck," Dutch said. "You had to be alert or he'd get you. If it was scared or mad, you never knew."

Once the bucking started the cowboy's sole aim was to "stay on top. You could be working out 10 miles and be walking home if you fell off."

Fire, wild hogs and snakes could set off a horse. Especially a nest of yellow jackets. "The cattle would stir them up," recalled Link, "and if they swarmed on your horse you were in for a ride."

The ranch horse had to be surefooted on ranges dotted with gopher, squirrel and raccoon holes. It had to be able to cut a single cow out of a crowded herd at roundup time. It learned to get its rider in the best roping position and apply the brakes to control an anxious steer.

"If you broke one," said Link, "and it worked well for you, you were proud of it and used it as much as you could."

*The ranch horse had to be surefooted on ranges dotted with gopher, squirrel and raccoon holes*

### ROPING

On the range the cowboy's essential tool was his lariat. The Wilsons used a 35-foot grass rope and spent practically every spare moment perfecting the art of roping.

"You had to be able to catch a steer with the first loop," said Dutch. "If you missed, you'd have to chase it another half mile before you'd get another crack."

During a roundup, roping cattle was usually a three-person operation performed in the confines of a corral. One rider looped the animal by its horns (heading), another tied its heels (heeling) and a third pulled the steer to the ground—often by its tail. But when chasing a stray calf in open country the solitary cowboy resorted to hog-tying. After roping the animal's horns, the cowboy looped the other end of the rope around his saddle horn (dallying). While his horse held the line taut, the ranch hand picked up and threw the 150 to 300-pound calf to the ground.

To practice, cowboys tossed their lariats at anything on the trail—bushes, tree limbs, rocks. The best way to practice was to chase and rope the cattle, "but you didn't want the boss to know it," said Link. "They didn't want you to run the fat off them, and if you roped them outside the corral they would tend to get a little wild."

Once the Wilsons and a buddy snuck into a corral and timed themselves with a stopwatch as they practiced heading, heeling and throwing cattle "until we got caught and had to stop it," Link recalled.

### RODEOS

Dutch still had the number he wore at a Salinas Rodeo in the 1930s, plus buckles and other prizes he won at rodeos in his youth.

"Rodeo has progressed like the Super Bowl," he said. "They were a dime a dozen. Now it's big money and big payoffs."

"In 1935 at the Salinas Rodeo, it was $7.50 a man for roping with a $500 purse. In the 1980s it's $250 a man for team roping with a purse of about $80,000."

Rodeos used to be spur-of-the-moment affairs, Link recalled.

"In small towns, somebody would bring in some bucking stock and you'd have yourself a rodeo. There were no chutes for the horses. You'd put sacks (called "blinds") over their eyes, saddle 'em, get on and turn 'em loose. All we had for fences were our cars."

At the end of the rodeo a hat was passed to pay the riders.

In those days money obviously was not the object of the exercise. It was entertainment and an opportunity "to show that you could do something a little better than the next guy," said Dutch.

"It was like baseball players. Every one wasn't a major leaguer. It was the same with cowboys, too."

*By Bob Nelson, June 1987*

# LAST OF THE
# CATTLE DRIVES

In the years between the two world wars, the task of the cattleman was revolutionized when a newfangled contraption—the truck—rolled onto the ranch. Large cattle trucks dramatically reduced the time required to get a herd to market. Where once it took days for the rancher on horseback to drive a herd to the nearest railhead, suddenly the cattle could be weighed at the ranch, loaded on trucks and sent to the packers in an afternoon.

The days of the cattle drive—romanticized in American literature and film—abruptly ended, to be recalled over the decades by a dwindling number of ranchers. One is Winston Wickenden, of pioneer Benjamin Foxen stock, who as a teenager joined his father in 27-mile drives from their ranch in Foxen Canyon east of Santa Maria to the train in Guadalupe.

Wickenden was 15 in the summer of 1920 when he and two high school friends were roused one midnight to help 10 cowboys gather cattle for that year's drive. By 6 a.m. the herd had been weighed and the men, boys and animals began the long procession to Guadalupe.

At 88, Wickenden clearly recalled the events of those summer days. His story, told in his own words, embodies the experience of every Central Coast rancher of that era in a dusty, exhausting, sometimes-dangerous undertaking ...

The cattle were spread out for about a mile. We had a chuck wagon that brought the food and had a place for the cook to sleep and all that, pulled by two horses. We got as far as Fugler Point (near Garey). There were big corrals, and we planned to house our cattle there all night. We fed and watered them, locked the pens and spread a bail of hay on the ground, covered it with a canvas, and there the cowboys slept.

**Young Winston Wickenden, left, helps load a herd into a cattle car.**
*Photo/Santa Maria Valley Historical Society*

Around midnight the cattle buyer arrived and woke us all, saying we had to get up and start moving the cattle. He said there was a special freight train going south into Los Angeles, and if we could make that train by noon and have our cattle loaded, the cattle would be in Los Angeles that evening.

So we took off for Guadalupe, which we never should have done, going off in the dark like that. At two o'clock in the morning the front herd of those cattle was hit by a car driven by a Saturday night drunk coming back from a party or something. Smashed right into the steers. Didn't kill any but injured some and started a stampede—the cattle broke in all directions.

I was bringing up the rear. My father came running back to me and yelled, "The steers are stampeding! Get behind a telephone post and let 'em go by!" About 50 or 70 were heading to the rear, and they all rushed by me. I couldn't stop 'em, and they could have run over me in the dark. After I got back to my senses I got on a horse and went out to bring them back.

It took several hours before we were able to get the steers toned down. There were steers up in the Telephone Road area—that's the Lake Marie area today. There were steers down in the Santa Maria River bed and scattered all over. Our count showed we were 17 short, but we took what he had and headed again to Guadalupe.

We came up Stowell Road, and when we got up as far as the cemetery area (intersecting College Drive) my father sent me and my two friends ahead to stop all the traffic at Broadway and Stowell. It was just a two-lane street at that time. When somebody drove up, we crossed our horse sideways so they would stop, and the other cars would pull up behind. It didn't take long, less than an hour. Of course, if we tried to do that today we'd all get killed.

When we got across we approached an old beet field, and along the edge of the fence inside the beet field were our 17 steers—they were all bawling, calling out to their friends. Those steers had come through at night, crossed Broadway, and were waiting for us to come through!

When we came to the outskirts of Guadalupe it was about noon. Of course we were late and missed the train that was coming through to take our cattle. The Southern Pacific had huge cattle corrals there and loading chutes, and that's where we housed the steers.

All the cowboys rode into Guadalupe, tied up their horses at the lampposts and sat down for lunch at what is now the Far Western restaurant. No sooner had we started our lunch when the cattle buyer burst in and said another train was pulling out from Pismo and would be there in a half hour, and we had to get back and start loading the steers.

We cut steers out in carload lots and herded them over to the loading chute. The train would spot a car, the doors would be opened and up the stairs and in they would go,

My father came running back to me and yelled, 'The steers are stampeding! Get behind a telephone post and let 'em go by!'

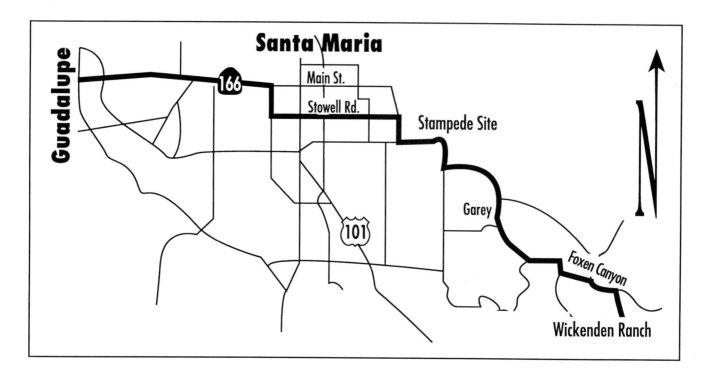

**Route of the cattle drive from the Wickenden Ranch in Foxen Canyon to the railroad in Guadalupe.**

about 30 for each car. Then the brakeman would slam the doors closed, latch them, signal to the engineer, and he would pull up another car. We were through about 6 o'clock that evening, and the train pulled out for Los Angeles.

The cattle probably brought around $200 a piece—200 cattle would be $40,000. The buyer gave my father a check right there in Guadalupe.

The cowboys spread their hay down and took out their canvas again and decided to stay all night. I got permission from my father to go home. It was just getting dark when my friends and I started out, and we arrived at Foxen Canyon at two o'clock in the morning. We were on horseback for 26 hours with the exception of the half hour when we gobbled up our lunch.

The poor horses had been going for 26 hours without stopping, too, and their legs were all stiff. They could hardly walk for a couple of days.

My father would always leave Guadalupe with the cowboys and stop at the (old) Bank of Santa Maria. It was right on the corner of Broadway and Main. He would go inside and deposit the check, then he would cross the street over to Whiskey Row, and at one of the bars all the cowboys would get drinks on the ranch. I was with him some of those times, and we boys would hold the horses in the street.

Once they got loosened up and thawed out, my father and the cowboys would come out of the bar, get on their horses, and away we would go trottin' back to the ranch.

*August 1993*

**A**S ANOTHER Lompoc Flower Festival drew near, Josie Manfrina and Harry Joy were inclined to reminisce.

They had spent many years in the Lompoc Valley, and their memories were keen. They recalled that a new shopping center was a golden field of marigolds not so long ago. They pointed out a housing complex that once was a cherry orchard crowded with blossoming trees.

They bemoaned the creeping urbanization and commercialization that was paving over fields once full of blooms.

However, most of the 100,000 visitors to the Flower Festival would not notice the difference. They would be entranced by more than 1000 acres blooming in brilliant shades of blue, pink, purple, scarlet and amethyst; the air would be fragrant with the scents of sweet alyssum and sweet peas.

Sometime during the parade through downtown or during the carnival at Ryon Park or Alpha Club Flower Show they would learn that the Lompoc Valley produced about half of the world's flower seed, a prodigious 400 tons a year. Citizens could boast that their community was the "Flower Seed Capital of the World."

But Josie Manfrina and Harry Joy could be forgiven for clutching the past: when the sweep of flower fields covered a full 2000 acres; when one 5-acre field of larkspurs bloomed into a red-white-and-blue American flag during World War II; when the Lompoc Valley produced *almost all* the world's

# LIFE
# IN LOMPOC'S
# FLOWER FIELDS

**A Lompoc flower field worker is surrounded by acres of blooms.**

flower seed.

Manfrina lived for years on a flower farm—"a breathtaking, fragrant existence," she said—and at age 16 was working summers in the Depression-era fields for 25 cents an hour.

Joy spent a half-century in the seed business in England and the U.S., 16 of them as manager of Denholm Seed Co. in Lompoc. He was an unofficial historian of the area's seed industry.

At the turn of the century, Joy said, most of the world's flower seed was grown and used in Europe. But W. Atlee Burpee was experimenting with seed production at a farm in Pennsylvania.

Lompoc's opportunity to raise flowers arrived almost by accident. A visiting Scotsman named John Smith suggested to local bean rancher Robert Rennie that he try growing some sweet peas, a plant in great demand in Europe.

The sweet peas thrived on a half acre of the Rennie Ranch (near present-day Central Avenue and H Street), and the success came to the attention of the Burpee Seed Co. in Philadelphia.

Burpee hastened to California and discovered that the Lompoc Valley's ocean breezes were ideal for pollination. It was warm during the day and cool at night; good water and soil were plentiful.

Soon hundreds of acres around Rennie's Ranch were in flower seed production. By the 1920s there were other seed companies cultivating valley land—Zvolanek, Denholm, Bodger.

"The farmers welcomed it," said Joy. "It was a change from beans and barley and sugar beets.

"They liked sweet peas ... they were getting about 50 cents a pound, and they could produce 400-500 pounds of seeds per acre."

They also liked nasturtiums, marigolds, petunias, zinnias, larkspur, delphinium, poppies, stock and other varieties, 500 in all.

Planting took place during December and January, and by June several hundred workers were in the fields. In 1932, Manfrina spent summer days pollinating petunias with a camel hair brush.

"They (the petunias) wouldn't produce seeds by themselves," she recalled. "We opened the blossoms and took the pollen from the male to the female."

Seated on a stool, she moved quickly from plant to plant, returning four or five times during June to pollinate new blossoms.

A double-blossomed petunia was a special find. Manfrina used tweezers to cross-pollinate the doubles with other less-productive flowers to create double seeds.

Once she walked through rows of marigolds, pulling off the petals and smelling them. Her employer, Burpee, was searching for a then-unheard of odorless marigold.

Manfrina never found one of the prized flowers but

*Lompoc's opportunity to raise flowers arrived almost by accident*

someone in China did, and it was cross-pollinated with Lompoc marigolds to produce the odorless varieties available today.

Harvest began in late July and continued into October. Manfrina spent days picking seed pods from dried flowers, filling large buckets. The contents were emptied onto large sheets of canvas for further drying.

In other fields, flowers were cut, windrowed and collected for drying.

Japanese and later Filipino laborers used broom-like "flails" to thrash and beat the dried seed pods, separating the seed from the kernel. Dirt and debris were removed before the seed was packaged for shipping to wholesale customers.

At its peak in the 1950s and 1960s, Burpee had 4 million customers for its catalog seed business and hundreds of wholesale clients. Lompoc's 2000 acres of flowers overwhelmed the 100 or so acres in production in other parts of the country. The Lompoc Valley produced fully 70 percent of the world's flower seed.

But over the succeeding two decades the world began to catch up, and so did the demands of a growing valley.

Nations in Central America and North Africa, their labor and land costs low, challenged Lompoc's pre-eminent position in the seed industry. Burpee Seed Co., long ago sold to a multinational corporation, closed its Lompoc operation. Truck crops and housing tracts replaced flowers on hundreds of acres.

Demand for flower seed is down, Joy explained.

"In general, it is the attitude of the general gardening public in years of affluence," he said. "Now people tend to

**At its peak, the Lompoc Valley produced 70 percent of the world's flower seed.**

*Photos/Lompoc Valley Historical Society*

buy plants grown at a nursery instead of buying seeds and waiting for them to grow.

"And people have other interests," he added. "They have summer homes and they travel more. They're leaving the gardening work to gardeners."

But the future does not appear grim, only different.

Mechanization controls costs. The marigold seeds Manfrina picked by hand are now removed by giant vacuum harvesters. Flailing machines have replaced humans.

"There will always be sweet peas, nasturtiums and a few other annuals grown here," Joy said.

Greenhouses will continue to thrive. "More and more work will be done under glass," Joy said, "and we will have more and more controlled production of hybrid items—exotic things."

So the colors and fragrances will remain in Lompoc for the enjoyment of future Flower Festival visitors and the reminiscing of those with unbreakable ties to an even more colorful and fragrant past.

*By Bob Nelson, June 1986*

T HERE IS LITTLE to disturb the shifting majesty of the Guadalupe Dunes these days.

Once a playground for hundreds of dune buggy drivers and campers, the massive sand hills west of Santa Maria now are crossed only by an occasional hiker or fisherman, or by cattle from ranches that surround the dunes.

Otherwise, the only companion for the Guadalupe Dunes is the wind, which alters the sandy landscape with each daily breeze.

Nothing disturbs the spot where, in 1923, legendary moviemaker Cecil B. DeMille brought together 2,500 people and 3,000 animals for the filming of the silent epic *The Ten Commandments*.

On the site, DeMille constructed a huge set for the Egyptian pharaoh's city. Considered one of the "great sets" from Hollywood's gaudy early years, the walled city was 750 feet long and at least 100 feet high.

Six decades later, a Los Angeles filmmaker poked around the dunes for traces of the DeMille set. "If what we have been told is true, and it seems to be true," said Peter Brosnan, "the set is indeed there."

Brosnan, with the assistance of archaeologists and local ranchers, hoped to unearth the buried remains of the *Ten Commandments* set as part of a documentary film on the silent movie.

For Brosnan, it was the climax to a detective story in which a series of clues led him to an archaeological treasure

# DeMille's Mystery City in the Dunes

**Cecil B. DeMille's set for the pharaoh's city constructed in the Guadalupe Dunes was 750 feet long and at least 100 feet high.**

long forgotten.

"There is a time when things like this set are not useful and they become old and obsolete and are thrown away," he said. "But after a time they become artifacts and are valuable."

For Clarence Minetti, a co-owner of the dunes area and longtime rancher and restaurateur in the Santa Maria Valley, it was a shock. "I had no idea all that stuff was buried there," he said.

"We were running cattle all the time right through there from our ranch to one of the others. What I have seen looks weather-beaten and decrepit ... a bunch of plaster of Paris with the wind blowing through it."

Minetti remembered that his father in-law was a partner in the deal that provided the thousands of animals for *The Ten Commandments*. And he recalled seeing giant sphinx statues from the set decorating a valley ranch and standing at the entrance to what is now the Santa Maria Country Club.

But that was decades ago. Those few traces of the mighty set were long gone when Minetti heard of Brosnan's project.

Only a self-proclaimed "film nut" like Brosnan would invest the time to track down the lost movie set. But he was intrigued by a tale told by his friend and fellow film aficionado Bruce Cardozo.

'We were amazed to find a large mound of garbage from an earlier period covered over by dirt and sand'

"Bruce was telling me this unbelievable story about Cecil B. DeMille burying sphinxes in the Guadalupe Dunes," Brosnan said. "It was just unbelievable enough to cause me to make a couple of calls."

And Brosnan read DeMille's autobiography, where he found this tell-tale paragraph:

If a thousand years from now archaeologists happen to dig beneath the sands of the Guadalupe Dunes, I hope they will not rush into print with the amazing news that Egyptian civilization, far from being confined to the valley of the Nile, extended all the way to the Pacific coast of North America. The sphinxes they will find were buried there when we had finished with them and dismantled our huge set of the gates of Pharaoh's city ...

With this and other clues, Brosnan and Cardozo visited the dunes. "We were amazed to find a large mound of garbage from an earlier period covered over by dirt and sand," he said.

Brosnan was convinced that the entire set is buried in the sand. "And sand is a good preservative," he added.

He hoped to work out details with Minetti and his partners, the Santa Maria Valley Associates, as well as the California Coastal Commission and other agencies in order to begin excavation.

He expected to find some of 22 sphinxes (each 15 feet long, seven feet high and weighing two tons) plus statues and other artwork that were part of the set. Film shot during the excavation was to become part of a documentary about the making of *The Ten Commandments*, which along with *King of Kings*, *Intolerance* and *Cleopatra* gave Hollywood its "great sets" of the silent era.

"This set was far bigger than anything built before or since," Brosnan said. "It was at a time when Hollywood was getting in gear and just hitting its stride, putting out a product that was bringing a positive image of America to the world.

"It gave Hollywood that bigger-than-life image."

Brosnan said DeMille likely chose the Guadalupe Dunes over more-accessible beaches in Southern California because "none had the great expanse Guadalupe offered. Understand, he needed a place to build an entire city."

Some of what Brosnan finds would be donated to the Hollywood Heritage Museum. And Santa Maria may be interested in some of the relics. "The set is part of its heritage," Brosnan said.

"It is more than memorabilia," he added, "because these are the last remaining pieces of the great sets. They are more like artifacts ... of historical importance.

"They should be preserved because when they are gone there will nothing like them again."

*By Bob Nelson, originally published in September 1983*

**Note: Brosnan's search produced bursts of local interest and a few exciting discoveries, but as this book went to press most of the DeMille set's secrets and memorabilia remained buried in the dunes.**

**Sphinxes from the famed set stood for years at the entrance to the Santa Maria Country Club.**
*Photos/Santa Maria Valley Historical Society*

# ALLAN HANCOCK AND THE 'SOUTHERN CROSS'

OTHING ROARED LOUDER during the Roaring Twenties than the engines of the world's pioneer flyers.

Aviation was a perfect complement to that gaudy era. Only two decades had passed since the Wright Brothers' watershed flight, and the sky offered limitless opportunity and adventure to anyone with the curiosity and courage to probe it.

One event, Charles Lindbergh's 1927 solo flight across the Atlantic Ocean, captured the world's imagination and made the young pilot a national hero. There were other oceans to be crossed, though—the Pacific being the most alluring. And a visionary Central Coast man was instrumental in the conquest of the largest ocean.

The challenge of crossing the Pacific consumed the ambition of a 31-year-old Australian, Capt. Charles Kingsford-Smith, known to most as "Smithy." A former World War I flying ace, Kingsford-Smith by early 1928 had crossed the Atlantic from east to west (reversing Lindbergh's direction) and completed a 7500-mile flight around Australia.

In March, Kingsford-Smith and his friend and co-pilot, Capt. Charles T.P. Ulm, were in Los Angeles making plans to fly from California to Australia in a rebuilt three-motor plane, the *Southern Cross*.

Their preparations were dogged by public wariness and a lack of funding. Earlier attempts to reach Hawaii in single-engine craft were disasters; at least four men died in the attempts and opinion soured on the possibility of a trans-Pacific flight.

At the same time a change in government in Australia eliminated the aviators' political and financial backing. The *Southern Cross* was about to be auctioned to pay debts.

At the depth of his despair, Kingsford-Smith was introduced to Capt. G. Allan Hancock, a wealthy industrialist with vast holdings in Los Angeles and Santa Maria—a man with an intense interest in aviation.

Hancock had learned to fly years earlier and was accustomed to making routine hops from his field in Santa Maria to Los Angeles and San Francisco. He was preparing to turn the Santa Maria field into one of the nation's first schools for pilots.

The first meeting of the flyers and the industrialist was uneventful. But a few days later Kingsford-Smith and Ulm received a surprise invitation to join Hancock on a 12-day cruise to Mexico aboard Hancock's yacht.

After 10 days at sea, Hancock was ready to talk business. As Kingsford-Smith later related in his book, *Story of the Southern Cross*:

"Suddenly he asked us what were our plans, and how much money did we need to get us out of our unenviable position. We told him frankly that we needed $16,000 to solve the problem.

"Then came the light in the darkness.

"I'll buy the machine from you boys," said Capt. Hancock. "I'll see my attorneys and decide what is the best method to follow in doing it."

In a book about Hancock, *A Pioneer Heritage*, author Sam T. Clover gives the incident a more romantic flair:

"It was not until the hour of parting came when Capt. Hancock remarked quietly, following a friendly handshake: 'You are going to fly to Australia in the *Southern Cross*. I don't know just how, yet, but we will take the matter up later. Rest assured, however, that you are going.'"

Hancock's motivation?

"It was an adventure for him, a challenge," said his wife, Marian. "It was right after Lindbergh, and aviation needed a shot in the arm."

Kingsford-Smith now had a backer—one who insisted on doing things right. The *Southern Cross* was saved from the auctioneer and overhauled. Hancock convinced the aviators to add an experienced navigator and radioman to their crew. He commissioned a film to be produced for the flight.

The *Southern Cross*, a high-winged Fokker monoplane with a 71-foot wingspan, was a sturdy craft once used for arctic exploration. Its three Wright Whirlwind engines gave the plane a high speed of 120 mph; Kingsford-Smith throttled back to 90 mph to give him a maximum of 41 hours in the air before refueling.

**Making possible the historic flight of the *Southern Cross* was just one of many projects undertaken by Santa Maria industrialist G. Allan Hancock.**

Some work was performed in Santa Monica, some in Santa Maria. Early on the morning of May 31, 1928 the *Southern Cross*, painted bright blue and crowded with fuel and supplies, lifted off into the fog from Oakland Airport and headed west. Hancock, incognito, observed the takeoff from the crowd.

Twenty-seven hours later the plane landed in Honolulu, ending the "easiest" leg of the journey. The aviators refitted, refueled and took off for the small island of Suva in the Fiji Islands, 3100 miles and 34 hours away.

They survived a series of crises: heavy rains and rough air pummeled the aircraft; the radio died; an engine began misfiring; a special compass failed. A slight error in navigation would have sent them away from Fiji, just a speck in the horizon, and to oblivion.

The *Southern Cross* found Suva and its 400-yard grass airstrip on June 5 and on June 8 departed for the hair-raising 1500-mile final leg through violent storms to Brisbane, Australia.

The historic flight ended at 10:50 a.m. June 9 when the *Southern Cross* touched down in Brisbane to a welcoming mob of 15,000 Australians. In a little over 83 hours, Kingsford-Smith and his crew had covered 7357 miles.

On their arrival, the aviators were handed a cable from Hancock, congratulating them and releasing them from their debt, in effect returning the *Southern Cross* to them.

With their own plane, plus $100,000 raised by admiring fans, the crew set off on an around-the-world flight. The *Southern Cross* continued to London, Ireland, Newfoundland, New York and Oakland.

On July 8, 1930 the Southern Cross landed at Hancock Field to be greeted by their benefactor and hundreds of Santa Marians.

Those heady days were the high-water mark of Kingsford-Smith's career. The flight of the *Southern Cross* never received the world-wide acclaim given to the Lindbergh flight, as trans-Atlantic and trans-Pacific flights became increasingly commonplace.

Smithy continued to pioneer until he disappeared with his plane, the *Lady Southern Cross*, over the Indian Ocean on Nov. 6, 1935 during a flight from England to Australia. But he died with the knowledge that his feats had set the stage for a dramatic shrinking of the Pacific for air travel.

The *Southern Cross*, revered in Australia, is on display in a museum in that nation. For the Central Coast, there is a scale model of the *Southern Cross* in the Santa Maria Valley Historical Museum.

For Capt. G. Allan Hancock, breaking the Pacific barrier was just one more success in a life of accomplishment. The site of the return of the *Southern Cross* became the Hancock College of Aeronautics, a prestigious pilot-training center, and later Allan Hancock College.

But he could always point with pride to a radio message

*The* Southern Cross *touched down in Brisbane to a welcoming mob of 15,000 Australians*

**Crowds jammed the tiny Santa Maria airfield for the return of the *Southern Cross*.**

sent by Kingsford-Smith after leaving Fiji:

"Now that we are sure of success, we wish to announce to the world that we could never have made this flight without the generosity and wonderful help given us by Capt. Allan Hancock. For months we had fought against giving up all hope, but we were practically counted out when we met Capt Hancock, who in a most unselfish manner saw us through."

*By Bob Nelson, September 1985*

# THE NAVY'S DEATH RIDE AT HONDA POINT

THE PRE-DAWN FOG hung heavily over the Douglass farm southwest of Lompoc on Sunday, September 9, 1923 as 17-year-old Anderson Douglass flung on clothes for a day trip to the beach.

It was to be no ordinary journey to the shore. A few hours earlier, word of a shipping accident at Honda Point—also known as "The Devil's Jaw"—had galloped through Lompoc. "News was that a battleship went aground," remembered Douglass, who was determined to be among the first at the scene.

With a friend, Douglass drove west to Surf, parked and trudged south three miles along the coastline toward Honda. They arrived just as the rising sun burned through a layer of fog.

"I first saw one boat," he recalled, "and when we walked a little further I saw a whole bunch of 'em. One boat was upside-down. The sailors were up on the rocks, shivering, cold and wet—in shock, I guess. It was quite a sight."

He was not looking at battleships but destroyers—nine of them floundering on razor-sharp rocks as far as the eye could see. A nighttime navigational error had sent the ships straight into The Devil's Jaw. Twenty-three men died and dozens were injured in the greatest peacetime disaster in the annals of the U.S. Navy.

It began early Saturday, September 8, when a column of 14 destroyers, among the Navy's newest and fastest warships, left San Francisco on a speed test to San Diego. The commander of each vessel was expected to follow the course

**A destroyer lies helpless after running aground at Honda Point.**

and pace set by the lead ship, the *Delphy*.

By nightfall, as fog thickened and the sea grew rough, the column approached Point Arguello and Point Conception, part of a 21-mile stretch of coastline known to sailors as the "Graveyard of Ships." At least 50 ships have been wrecked since 1815 in the rock-guarded, windswept area thought by some to be the home of evil spirits and sailors' ghosts. The Devil's Jaw, where rolling waves conceal the rocks, is smack in the middle of this West Coast version of the Bermuda Triangle.

The column of destroyers was expected to steam past the Graveyard and execute a left turn into the Santa Barbara Channel, where the coast takes a long eastward sweep before swinging back southward toward Los Angeles and San Diego.

The officers of the *Delphy*, running at a crisp 20 knots, could not see landmarks or stars in the thickening fog. By dead reckoning, based on compass course and speed, they determined that the ship was just south of Point Conception and ready for the turn into the Santa Barbara Channel. The commander ignored a signal from an often-unreliable radio compass station on Point Arguello which indicated that the vessel was still well north of the channel entrance.

Just before 9 p.m., the *Delphy* made a hard left turn—and plowed into the rocks of The Devil's Jaw. One by one, eight other destroyers followed the lead ship into the Graveyard.

The following hours were a nightmare of death, injury, panic and bravery as sailors struggled on listing decks and through rolling, oil-covered surf to rescue themselves and their shipmates. Most did not realize how close they were to shore until dawn broke.

A worker at a Southern Pacific Railroad depot near Honda heard the crash and first spread the alarm. At about 10 o'clock it reached Lompoc, where most of the citizenry was attending a public dance at the old Opera House.

"I remember my dad took off with some other men and drove down that night," said Charlotte McClellan, another member of the pioneer Douglass family. "They couldn't see anything, but they could hear men calling for help. They stayed for a couple of hours but couldn't do anything."

The next morning Charlotte, her mother and sister packed a lunch and went to the crash site. "It was unbelievable," she said. "Some of the ships were still on the rocks—one was practically onshore. The sailors who were able to get out were on the rocks calling for help, and men on the shore were throwing ropes to them to bring them to shore. They were covered with oil. Doctors were caring for them as best they could. Some men were dead in the water or had washed ashore."

By that time her cousin Anderson Douglass and his friends had arrived and made their way to the *Chauncey*, the wreck nearest shore, by means of a rigged rope chair and pulley system.

*The* Delphy *made a hard left turn—and plowed into the rocks of The Devil's Jaw*

**Onlookers watch from shore as stricken ships are smashed against the rocks.**

*Photos/Lompoc Valley Historical Society*

"It was pretty scary," he recalled. "There was quite a hole in its side; you could see it when the swells went down.

"We went below deck and crawled around the bunks. A lot of the area was underwater. All of a sudden it was announced over the loudspeaker for all civilians to get ashore, so we got."

Navy officials arrived to set up a tent mortuary near the Southern Pacific tracks, and Shore Patrol units kept the public away from the stricken vessels. By midday a traffic jam was forming in the Lompoc area as people from Santa Maria to Santa Barbara arrived to gawk at the wrecks. Some visitors brought blankets for bone-chilled sailors who waited to be taken by train to San Diego.

Eerily, a solar eclipse occurred in the early afternoon—a sign of delight, perhaps, from the evil spirits of the Graveyard.

Douglass and his friends watched the macabre proceedings until late in the day. "Sometimes you'd see porpoises pushing bodies ashore," he said. "It was a squeamish sight to see."

The death toll of 23 was surprisingly low for such a calamity. Two destroyers were freed from the rocks; seven sank.

Today, at low tide, one can see the remains of the Chauncey from Honda Point, now part of Vandenberg Air Force Base. A marker and a rusty anchor are the only memorials at the largest burial plot in the Graveyard of Ships.

*By Bob Nelson, October 1988*

*People dream of being on a South Seas island, living off the land and not having to go out and hustle. It was right here in our backyard.*
**—Norm Hammond**

T HE DUNES OF the Central Coast conceal much of their essence. They envelop mile after isolated mile of coastline, the blowing sand altering the topography nearly every day. A person—even a group of people—can vanish into the broad expanse.

In the early decades of this century, a group of mystics, hobos and free spirits disappeared into the sandy hills south of Oceano. The colony thrived in the woody thickets deep inside the dunes, protected from the ocean breezes and free from prying eyes and the constraints of the modern world.

They called themselves The Dunites.

The Dunites vanished from their retreat in the 1940s—as quickly and quietly as they had arrived. They might have been forgotten but for the efforts of Norm Hammond, a San Luis Obispo firefighter and a self-styled writer, artist and "duneophile."

For decades Hammond chronicled The Dunites, and his findings filled a manuscript that was eventually published.

Researching the volume "filled a need in my personal life," said Hammond, as comfortable in the silent recesses of the dunes as in the workaday world.

"Basically, I'm one of those people," he explained. "Once I found out about it (the Dunite encampment), researching it allowed me to live there myself vicariously."

Born in Arizona and raised in Wyoming, Hammond settled on the Central Coast in 1967 and began hiking the dunes. "Intuitively I knew there had been people there," he recalled. "I saw that the area was custom made, with water and food."

He came across old bottles and cans and other evidence of previous habitation. And during one trek he stumbled upon the cabin of the last dune resident, Bert Schievink, who had lived a hermit's life in the sand for more than 30 years.

Schievink rebuffed Hammond's attempt to ask questions (he died in 1974) but spurred the writer into a decade-long search for The Dunites.

He discovered a loosely knit group that began filtering into the dunes after the Spanish-American War and peaked in size during the Great Depression of the 1930s.

At that high point, three distinct types of people could be found: hobos looking for a temporary layover during their search for work; mystics who found the dunes ideal for studying astrology, philosophy, religion, even black magic; and short and long-term escapees from society.

They lived in cabins and shelters constructed from driftwood and pieces of abandoned beachfront buildings. Their diet consisted primarily of clams found in profusion along the beach and vegetables swiped from nearby fields.

# THE DUNITES: A UTOPIAN SOCIETY IN THE SAND

**A Polynesian-style hut was the domain of Dunite George 'Nature Boy' Blais.**

*Photo/The Gerber Collection*

The more sociable Dunites occasionally appeared in Oceano to pick up mail and groceries.

Foremost among The Dunites was the group led by Chester Alan Arthur—known to most as Gavin Arthur—the grandson of 19th century President Chester Arthur. His colony congregated in an area dubbed "Moy Mell," a Gaelic expression meaning "Pasture of Honey," located in a willow thicket about two miles south of Pier Avenue in Oceano.

"He was trying to create a utopia," said Hammond. Moy Mell attracted "free thinkers, artistic people who simply wanted to be free."

They also wanted to be entertained, and Gavin Arthur "brought money into the dunes," Hammond said. "He was a gregarious person, and anybody who lived down there knew him and liked him.

"Of course, Gavin was a great party-er. Napoleon brandy and all the best was always at his place."

The liquor was free, so was the food, and the climate was ideal. As many as 30 people occupied Moy Mell during the 1930s and adhered to a lifestyle that would be emulated by beatniks and hippies of later generations.

There was Hugo Seelig, "The Poet," who never intended to see his work in print. And there was George "Nature Boy" Blais, who wore only a loincloth and lived off hog grain from the Oceano feed store.

Ella Young was a mystic poetess and gunrunner during the Irish Revolution. Emily Wingate was a cover girl for *Vogue* magazine. Dozens of other free spirits came and went.

They published *The Dune Forum*, a monthly literary journal that survived only seven issues but supposedly came to the attention of John Steinbeck, W.C. Fields and thousands of others interested in the Dunite culture.

In his search Hammond found Elwood Decker, an artist and writer who had spent 13 years in the dunes. He cautioned Hammond: "Do not become attached to the beauty of the dunes and all their little creatures. Remember that basically everything is just an illusion ..."

For The Dunites, the illusion dissolved soon after America entered World War II. "The Coast Guard came in, toting pistols and gun bandoliers," Hammond said. "The whole thing took the edge off this place."

Moy Mell was quickly abandoned, Gavin Arthur returned to San Francisco, and the dunes were left to a few solitary souls like Bert Schievink.

Years later Hammond arrived to pick up the pieces of dunes lore and write a book, *The Dunites*.

But even Hammond stopped going to the site of Moy Mell after he was struck by a motorcycle, one of the off-road vehicles that intrude into the isolation of the dunes.

Is there space for a Dunite today?

"Oh yeah," said Hammond. "I've got places that I have discovered out there, and I can go camping out there and nobody can find me. It can happen."

Besides, the Dunite culture was much less a place than a state of mind. As *The Dune Forum* once proclaimed: "You don't have to live in the dunes to be a Dunite."

*By Bob Nelson, originally published in July 1985*

**Note: Norm Hammond's book, *The Dunites*, published in 1992 by the South County Historical Society, is available at the Halcyon Store and other Central Coast bookstores.**

# SECTION III

## MODERN TIMES
## 1940-PRESENT

# Camp Cooke: Proving Ground for War

**F**ROM LATE 1939 into mid-'41, American leaders stood aghast as a tank-led German juggernaut smashed through Europe and North Africa. They realized that the U.S. was woefully unready to battle the German tank menace. Entire divisions had to be created from scratch to fight the looming war against Hitler.

In a frantic search for armored forces training areas, Washington's eye fell upon land near the mouth of the Santa Ynez River. The rolling terrain, even climate and nearness to the sea were ideal for a full spectrum of war maneuvers.

In less than a year, from mid-'41 through spring '42, the Lompoc Valley was transformed from sleepy farming community into bustling center of national defense. The change for the valley and nearby communities was permanent. And it was not without a price.

After surveys and a $17-million construction contract, the U.S. government condemned, then purchased, over 80,000 acres along 20 miles of coastline. The largest acquisition—41,000 acres—gutted Rancho Jesus Maria which dated back to a Spanish land grant. Another tract belonged to humorist-philosopher Will Rogers' son. The seaside hamlet of Surf became a ghost town, then a bulldozed sand dune.

Some unlucky landowners, after eviction from homes and ranches, languished unpaid for months as the federal bureaucracy struggled to keep up with the pace of war preparations.

Lompoc's townsfolk reeled when they learned the scope of Camp Cooke, named after Civil War general Philip St. George Cooke. Thirty-six thousand troops—more than ten times Lompoc's 1940 population—would occupy a new city. Plans for the mammoth base included railroad spurs and an airfield. There were to be nearly 500 barracks, a 1500-bed hospital, five chapels, water and sewer plants, and over 40 miles of roads. Two 1500-seat theaters and a 4000-seat sports arena would also be built.

The mouth of the Santa Ynez River would be partially blocked to prevent the ocean from salting Army wells.

In a briefing to citizenry, a well-meaning colonel tried to ease the deepest fears of some parents. "If your Lompoc girls get in trouble after the soldiers come," he declared, "it will be due either to liquor or lack of home training."

His audience was not reassured.

The Lompoc City Council enacted emergency ordinances to cope with the influx of job-hungry construction workers and their families. An army contract engineer warned: "... even if you built a high stone wall around the city, they still will get in ..." He went on to urge that city regulations "... can't be too strict."

City officials braced for an onslaught by gamblers and prostitutes which, as it turned out, was only a minor problem. Some crime did increase; trusting citizens were warned to lock their house doors and remove their keys from parked cars.

A swarm of 4500 civilian construction workers—tough union men—battled blinding dust, then muddy swamps, to erect the camp. Some days the blowing grit was so thick that heavy equipment operators lost their vehicles during lunch breaks. In the '41-'42 winter rains, entire caterpillar tractors were swallowed in muck, sinking from view as their drivers leapt to safety.

Enraged rattlesnakes, driven from their dens by the din, added to the confusion.

At the peak of construction, 14 trailer parks and a number of tent cities dotted the valley. Townsfolk opened their homes, and sometimes garages, to boarders; two or three to a room was the usual sleeping arrangement.

When the human wave of construction workers and their families receded, it was replaced by an avalanche of officers' wives and children.

While Lompoc begged for federal low-cost housing funds and struggled to meet the dwelling shortage, Santa Maria took a different tack. The newspaper and some civic leaders railed against the prospect of "socialistic housing."

Lompoc's famed flower industry slumped into hibernation. Most of the colorful acreage was drafted to grow vegetable seeds for America's "victory gardens." The sole exception—lifting spirits of townsfolk and soldiers alike—was Bodger Seed Company's patriotic floral flag.

Moore's department store spun off a military concession: uniforms sewn to order by the emporium's tailor. The Lompoc Theater on H Street advertised special box office rates for uniformed servicemen. The city's flagpole, in the middle of the intersection of H Street and Ocean Avenue, was uprooted to make room for the surge in traffic.

**Dances at the local USO Club were a popular diversion for Camp Cooke trainees and locals.**

Churches, fraternal societies and civic organizations like the Alpha Club threw open their doors to servicemen and their families. At the height of the war, three local USO clubs hosted the troops, even though soldiers were allowed off base only one night a week.

World-class celebrities such as Jimmy Durante, violinist Jascha Heifetz, Bob Hope, boxer Joe Louis, Babe Ruth and Rudy Vallee trekked to Lompoc to hearten the troops. Even the Three Stooges put in an appearance.

To cushion against the tidal waves of construction workers and soldiers, Washington shoveled money into the valley. By mid-'42, Lompoc had acquired a new sewer plant, water plant upgrades, school additions, a brand-new hospital, modern post office, low-cost federal housing projects, and an enormous USO building which became the postwar city hall. The town's cranky "number please?" manual switchboard faded into history, replaced by a dial system.

Despite the influx of federal funds, the upheaval was painful for many.

In late August '41, officers of Lompoc's Japanese-American Citizen's League were installed in a patriotic ceremony attended by the city mayor, a county supervisor, the Chamber of Commerce president and the local American Legion commander.

Then came December's Pearl Harbor shock.

By May '42, Roosevelt's powerful War Relocation Authority, declaring the entire area a prohibited zone, emptied Lompoc Valley of its Japanese-American citizens and confined them in bleak camps far from the coast. There followed a scramble to find another way to farm over 2000 acres which

**The Bodger Seed Company's patriotic floral flag.**

*Photos/Lompoc Valley Historical Society*

otherwise would be lost to the war effort.

Between '42 and '46, approximately 175,000 troops were dispatched from Camp Cooke, most to combat in the European Theater. Thousands of captured Germans and Italians were interned here in a prisoner-of-war camp. In a remote corner of the base stood a replica "Nazi village," booby-trapped to teach soldiers the nastier points of urban warfare.

Had atomic bombs not halted the war, Camp Cooke would have readied tens of thousands of soldiers for a gigantic amphibious invasion of Japan.

The clank of tank treads is silent now, replaced by the earthshaking roar of missiles. But Camp Cooke's wartime legacy survives on Vandenberg Air Force Base.

A war memorial honors the divisions that trained there. The monument, displaying a "Patton" tank, is sited not far from the old Army camp's headquarters.

Of the hundreds of the war's "temporary" wooden structures, many still stand today; the fire-prone, drafty buildings tax the ingenuity of Air Force civil engineers. The base is dotted with "Danger: Unexploded Ordnance" warnings near dozens of old artillery impact areas.

Camp Cooke is gone, but not forgotten.

*By Jon C. Picciuolo, July 1992*

# THE DEADLY FIGHTER CRASH ON BROADWAY

GUSTS OF WIND shivered in the dark gray clouds that gathered over Santa Maria on January 30, 1945, bringing hope that much-needed rain was on the way. But by noon the skies lightened enough for high-performance P-38 fighter planes to take off from the nearby Army airfield to practice maneuvers that soon would help end World War II.

At their Cook School playground, young Bill Allison and Gary McCabe enjoyed their 12:30 p.m. recess by watching the planes loop and dive through the sky. Allison often observed the pilots play their war games, and witnessed enough crashes that he could guess when a fighter was in trouble. As he watched an aircraft descend in a flat pattern and heard the screechy wheeze of the motor, he predicted, "That plane is going down, and it's headed straight to the middle of town."

Hearing the crash, young McCabe turned ashen. Racing toward the area where black smoke spiraled upward, he yelled, "My mother is working downtown at Woolworths!" Allison followed his friend McCabe, and the two will never forget the fiery carnage and the stench of burning flesh at South Broadway near Main Street.

The plane dropped from the south at an angle, ripped off the top of the rear of the Economy Drug store, and smashed into the wall of the Rusconi Cafe. The plane's gas tank exploded, blowing out the front window and allowing the proprietor, Filippo Rusconi, to escape. His wife, Tillie, and a cook, John Doff, were not so lucky—they were instantly killed. Parts from the tail snapped power lines, cutting off electricity to the area.

The dead pilot's hat was found nearby, causing some to speculate that Flight Officer Elmer Steffey was trying to jump from the plane just before it crashed. However, firemen reported his body was found in the cockpit.

To McCabe's relief, his mother was safe. Miraculously, there were only two additional injuries. Arthur Beall, who was unloading a truck in the alley behind the cafe, was cut on the forehead and nose by falling bricks, and W.H. Patterson, assistant manager of the drug store, was knocked to the floor by the explosion.

Quick action by the fire department contained the fire in the restaurant, but the neighboring Economy Drug Store and Bradley Hotel suffered water and smoke damage.

Yet, the danger from the skies was not over. Later the same day another P-38 plummeted to the ground near an Orcutt area ranch, killing the pilot, Flight Officer Robert E. Pettigrew.

Only two years before the local residents had rejoiced and celebrated when the Santa Maria Army Air Base was dedicated, but they now had grave concerns. Each day young pilots, fresh from only 16 hours of advanced instruction in single-engine trainers, practiced intricate maneuvers in the powerful and sophisticated twin-engine P-38s through the skies above the city.

With all the unoccupied land around the city and an entire ocean to the west, many questioned why the pilots had to play war games over populated areas. At least eight other P-38 crashes in surrounding areas already were documented.

Understanding the rising community indignation, Col. Burton M. Russell, commander of the base, announced his sincere regrets and stated, "I have instructed all pilots of this field that there will be no flying at any altitude over the City of Santa Maria."

According to Blanche Boardman Powell, who then worked at the Hancock Foundation College of Aeronautics, "My neighbors were relieved by Col. Russell's assurances. This was wartime and most people wanted to be hospitable to those pilots training to protect our country."

The day after the fatal crash into the Rusconi Cafe, dark clouds again blackened the sky, this time dumping more than an inch of rain. It caused the citizenry to wonder how things might have been different had the storm arrived 24 hours earlier.

*By Marilyn Schobel, February 1994*

**High-performance P-38 fighters regularly prowled the skies above Santa Maria during World War II. Many crashed, including one that rammed into the Rusconi Cafe, opposite.**

*Photos/Santa Maria Valley Historical Society*

Japanese-Americans on their way to wartime confinement.

*Photo/20th Air Force files*

# INTERNMENT: REMEMBERING WARTIME FEAR AND SHAME

TODAY CHILDREN often gather to play their noisy games on the front stone steps of the modest, gray First Buddhist Church on Olivera Street in Guadalupe.

In the spring of 1942, a much larger and very solemn group gathered in front of a more elaborate Buddhist church, 300 feet west on Guadalupe Street. There local Japanese-American families, holding only those things they could carry, fearfully awaited busses that would haul them to wartime internment camps.

On Mary Street in Santa Maria, another group of Japanese-Americans, with faces frozen by anxiety and anguish, also waited for the infamous transport vehicle. Toru Miyoshi was among them.

"The memory endures as a chilly reminder that any individual or group can be deprived of due process and carted away," recalled Miyoshi, today a Santa Maria city councilman and former Santa Barbara County supervisor.

"Americans must be alert that this could happen, especially in a time of crisis. We only can have a viable and cohesive community when open dialogue, not fear, is used as a solution to economic, social and political issues."

\*\*\*

Dialogue gave way to fear after Japanese airplanes bombed the American naval base at Pearl Harbor on December 7, 1941. Local FBI agents herded together astonished Japanese aliens, called *Issei*, and swiftly carried them off to detention areas away from the Central Coast.

Meanwhile, using the Japanese-American Citizen's League as their spokesperson, local Japanese-Americans condemned the attack and pledged complete loyalty to the United States. Many American-born Japanese already were in the military, and more immediately volunteered to teach their ancestral language to the armed forces.

To further prove its loyalty and cooperation, the JACL agreed to register all local Japanese-Americans and to gather their cameras, flashlights and radios—items considered dangerous to national security.

By February 1942, President Franklin D. Roosevelt's administration in Washington, D.C. had issued Executive Order No. 9066, allowing the removal of people from threatened areas "at the discretion of any appropriate military commander."

Officers in the United States Western Defense Command were jittery. Their job was to guard 1400 miles of coastline and to quickly investigate rumors of prowling Japanese planes, submarines and saboteurs.

In spite of FBI and other intelligence agencies stating there was little threat from Japanese-Americans, the Western Command decided to intern all Americans of Japanese heritage.

At the end of April, the shameful local odyssey from Guadalupe and Santa Maria began. Given 72 hours to gather together only items they could carry, many families were forced to sell their homes, farms and all other belongings at humiliating prices. Farmers reluctantly left crops already planted in the fields.

At the local boarding centers at the First Buddhist Church in Guadalupe and at a church on Mary Street in Santa Maria, the families were counted, tagged, crowded into busses, and swiftly delivered to temporary quarters in Tulare. Awaiting them were stuffy horse barns, surrounded by barbed wire and patrolled by soldiers carrying guns. The families lived crammed together with little privacy and anxiously wondering what would happen next.

*Given 72 hours to gather together only items they could carry, many families were forced to sell their homes, farms and all other belongings at humiliating prices*

\*\*\*

Paul Kurokawa was astounded when it was apparent his family would be moved to a relocation center.

"There is an old Japanese proverb that loosely translated says, 'It isn't the family that gives you birth, but the family that raises you to whom you owe your loyalty.' To assume the Japanese-Americans and the Japanese aliens would be disloyal is and was unthinkable," said Kurokawa, today a Guadalupe business and community leader.

"When I recall the experience, I remember most of us felt it was wartime and, if the government wanted us in internment camps, as loyal Americans we obeyed."

\*\*\*

After what seemed an eternity at Tulare, the interned Japanese-American families from the Santa Maria Valley were moved again, most to one of two camps in Arizona. Long lines of shade-drawn railroad cars carried them through suffocating heat. Inside the jammed and sultry cars, some children, excited by the new adventure, played together quietly; others sobbed softly on their mothers' shoulders. Resigned to their fate, the adults hoped things would be better once they arrived at the new destination.

What sounded like splattering rain pelted the train as it came to a halt in the Arizona camps. They stepped from the railway cars into gusts of dust and sand, violently churned by the winds. Layers of the particles coated them and their baggage.

The clusters of barracks that soon became their homes were the same at most camps. The new, hastily finished buildings were parceled into 16-by-20-foot units for each entire family. With gaps in the floor and wall planking, sand slithered into the rooms, covering everything in its path. The internees sweltered in the summer and froze in the winter.

There was an acceptable mess hall, but the bathroom facilities, only one for four barracks, always were inadequate. With a shortage of doctors, the camp clinic employed young interns to treat illnesses. Many died from what was called "Valley Fever."

*Undaunted, the families began to put their lives together*

Undaunted, the families began to put their lives together. They gathered scrap wood to fill in open spaces in the walls and floors, and used blankets to parcel off sleeping areas. Soon they cooked in the mess hall, worked in the clinic, and helped to keep the area tidy. Trees were planted, children enrolled in schools, and afternoon and evening social activities relieved some of the discomfort.

Soon many families again were uprooted when the men volunteered to serve in the military, help farm the land in the Midwest or work in manufacturing plants away from the western states. Others were able to find temporary homes with friends or relatives in the East.

On the war front, the all-Japanese-American 442nd Regimental Combat team, fighting in Italy, became the most decorated regimental unit in American history.

*\*\*\**

Many local Japanese-Americans are extremely uncomfortable recalling their wartime experiences, especially with outsiders. Three finally agreed to share their memories, but insisted on anonymity:

• One of Santa Maria's leading agricultural executives recalled, "After the war, I was luckier than most. I was able to acquire acreage to farm in one of the central California valleys. Eventually I returned to my home in Santa Maria to raise my family and establish this company. This has been my community and, like most local Americans of Japanese heritage, I am determined to help the city successfully face its many changes and challenges."

• One of the city's prominent professionals shook his head as he recalled the internment. "I never could understand how any American could question our allegiance. From our youngest days we are taught devotion and loyalty to our families, our community and our nation. Our criminal record is negligible, and our community service record impeccable."

• Part of a family that owned a profitable company in Guadalupe, a retired businessman commented, "My parents accepted their internment as a way of serving in the war. Already middle aged, they were forced to leave everything they worked so hard for. After the war ended, they had to start all over again. I don't think I could have handled it."

***

After the war, many Japanese-Americans opted to settle in the East and Midwest. In the California legislature, there was an unsuccessful attempt to keep the internees from returning home. But those who came back to the Santa Maria Valley once more became active in the community.

In 1988 the federal government reimbursed all surviving Japanese-Americans $20,000 in what amounted to a national act of contrition to those who lost land, homes, farms, businesses, possessions and 3-1/2 years of productivity.

"The Japanese-American internment must be remembered as a tragic mistake, never to be repeated," said Councilman Miyoshi. "As we approach the 21st century, all Americans must carefully listen, hear, discuss and wisely weigh all special viewpoints and issues and then discover solutions that best serve the common goal."

*By Marilyn Schobel, February 1994*

107

# A One-Man FBI

WHEN BILL NOLAN manned a lonely FBI outpost in Santa Maria, he tracked about 50 cases at any given time—bank robberies, murders, prison escapes, etc. Many cases took weeks to solve, some months or years, and some were never closed. But, fortunately for Nolan, some cases closed themselves.

Such was the situation during World War II, when three soldiers confined to the stockade at Camp Cooke (now Vandenberg Air Force Base) slipped free and headed for home.

"They went over the hills to Guadalupe where they were going to catch a train," Nolan recalled. "But instead of waiting for the train they walked over to a farmhouse and gave themselves up. They had had enough going through all that country with the snakes, without water and getting blisters."

Nolan needed some easy cases because he was the only FBI agent on the Central Coast. Arriving as a young man in 1944, he worked a territory stretching from Gaviota Pass in the south to the northern limits of San Luis Obispo County. Not until 1959 did he receive assistance from the agency—one man.

Long retired from the agency, Nolan is a fountain of stories about the early FBI, when his office was an extra bedroom in his home.

"Mr. Hoover didn't like to spend a lot of money," he said of the FBI's longtime Director J. Edgar Hoover. "He'd go to Congress for appropriations and show that his money from fines, savings and recoveries had exceeded the total amount spent for the operation."

That cost-consciousness applied to transportation. FBI agents drove low-priced Fords, Chevrolets and Plymouths without air conditioning ("We could have used it in Paso Robles when it was 100 degrees," Nolan laughed) and not even a commercial radio ("When you were driving, all you could do was think about your cases.").

There was plenty of ground to cover, including 100 or so miles of coastline to be protected from enemy landing parties during World War II.

"They were worried about saboteurs landing like they did on the East Coast," Nolan said. "We contacted people who lived as close to the coast as possible and asked them if they saw something suspicious to contact us.

"We used to get calls about flashing lights, signals to ships. But we determined that they were just car lights and not signals."

Not only was Nolan responsible for intercepting saboteurs and working normal FBI investigations—forgeries, kidnappings, bank robberies—he also had jurisdiction at the government reservations of Camp Cooke and Camp Roberts on the Monterey County line.

"I would get things (at the camps) the local police usually handled, burglaries and sex offenses and things like that—

things the FBI had never taken part in," he said.

During the peak years of the war effort, each camp was packed with as many as 30,000 men. "The fellas at Camp Cooke had been in service for some time, had basic training and were a little better," Nolan said. "But at Roberts they were just out of the draft board ... some of them didn't like the discipline. It had the biggest camp stockade I ever saw—must have been 200 prisoners at a time in there."

Most of the residents of the stockades were men who had been absent without leave (AWOL). Some, like the trio in Guadalupe, stayed on the loose for only a few days.

The rest "were easy people to find," Nolan said. "When they'd go, they'd go home. Ordinarily, their families would be relatively cooperative. I'd tell them, 'Why not take him back and turn him in?' If he was AWOL he'd probably just get the stockade and be fined part of his pay, which wasn't much."

Also under Nolan's jurisdiction were prisoners of war, about 1500 Germans at Camp Cooke and a like number of Italians at Camp Roberts. They, too, had a tendency to stroll.

"The Germans were the elite from Rommel's army," Nolan said. "They were fenced in, but they could tunnel out in 20 minutes. They really didn't guard them that much.

"They escaped because they wanted to see how the other half lived. They were bored on the base. But they were careful not to commit a crime. They'd catch a freight and head for Los Angeles, and by the time they were picked up or they turned themselves in, they could say that they had seen Hollywood."

One POW, still wearing his prisoner's garb with a large "PW" painted on the back, roamed the streets of Hollywood for two days without attracting notice.

Finally, speaking badly broken English, "he turned himself in to a police officer," Nolan recalled. "The police officer asked him what for, and he had to turn around and show him his shirt with the big PW before he'd take him in.

"I never talked to a single one that wanted to go back to Germany," he added. "They'd already been in the war and had enough."

Nolan never worked completely alone. He could call on the military police for assistance on the bases, and local law enforcement officials also lent a hand. But at the time, he noted, Santa Maria had only a chief of police and eight men, plus four highway patrolmen, one deputy sheriff, a constable and justice of the peace.

The small-town atmosphere was not unlike his native Tennessee, where he was raised in a Victorian-style cottage that was later entered into the National Register of Historic Places.

Graduating in 1938 from Vanderbilt University, he was a classmate of one Fanny Rose Shore, who became better known as Dinah Shore.

He practiced law until war clouds gathered, then contem-

**Bill Nolan in the garb of an FBI agent of the 1940s.**

plated joining the Navy. But the dean of Vanderbilt's law school suggested he look into the FBI, which accepted only lawyers and accountants at the time but was desperately short of manpower.

Nolan mailed his application on December 6, 1941—the day before the Japanese attack on Pearl Harbor hurled the United States into war. On December 17 he received a note signed by Director Hoover requesting that he travel to Memphis for extensive interviews.

On February 3, 1942 a telegram—also with Hoover's signature—arrived with an offer to join the agency. The pay: $3,200 a year plus $5 a day for expenses. Not much, but "it was more than I was making practicing law," Nolan said.

Rushed through intensive training, he took his first assignment at a headquarters in Seattle, then was transferred to a Los Angeles office before moving to Santa Maria.

Hoover "ran a good organization," Nolan said. "When you went in the Bureau they told you ... foul up once and you were out.

"They pretty well controlled your life."

Each agent wore a snap-brim hat and carried a .38 caliber revolver in a hip holster under his conservative suit—no sport coats, loud ties or socks, nor moustaches, beards or long hair.

*Each agent wore a snap-brim hat and carried a .38 caliber revolver in a hip holster under his conservative suit*

"That was the image—they wanted us to look like young businessmen," Nolan said. "To people, the first agent they talk to is going to form an impression of the whole agency."

Nolan filed daily reports accounting for virtually every minute of his time. He was on call 24 hours; while on vacation he was required to stop at Western Union offices to check for messages.

He met Hoover only once, although his scrapbook contains numerous notes from the director—get-well wishes during an illness, congratulations at the birth of his two children, personal thanks for closing a difficult case.

The men at the Morro Bay Naval Station treated Nolan like the FBI boss himself when he visited the base commander during the war.

Nolan showed the guard his identification, "and another sailor got in the car with me," he recalled. "On the way over the sailor said, 'We've heard a lot about you' and 'It's nice to see you' and 'Never thought I'd get to meet you.'"

The treatment puzzled Nolan as well as the base commander, who was not used to providing escorts for FBI agents.

"He called the gate and asked the guard what was the last name logged in," Nolan recalled. "The guard said, 'J. Edgar Hoover, sir!'

"You see, we signed our ID cards on the side and Hoover signed at the bottom, and the guard read the wrong signature. The commander said, 'Imagine J. Edgar Hoover driving up here by himself in his own car just to see me!'"

The war ended, the camps disbanded, but Nolan's stack

of cases remained tall. However, it was not until 1960 that he was involved in his first and only gun battle.

An escapee from San Quentin Prison, where he was serving a life sentence, shot and killed a highway patrolman on the road between Los Angeles and Barstow. A massive manhunt tracked him to Shell Beach, where his wife and son lived.

Nolan and the local police cornered the convict, armed with a sawed-off shotgun, in a motel room. "We called on him to come out and he started shooting," Nolan recalled. "He shot the front windows out of the motel room.

"We fired in some tear gas and nothing happened. We called to him and he fired again. Remember, this man had sworn he would never be taken back to San Quentin alive."

Nolan called again, and the escapee said he would come out "but he was afraid the highway patrolmen were going to kill him. I told him it would be all right, and he left his gun and came out.

"He apologized to me for shooting at me. He said his wife had told him I was a square shooter and would not have shot at him."

(A post script: The convict never returned to San Quentin; he was executed for the murder of the highway patrolman.)

Nolan's stay on the Central Coast, originally planned for one year, stretched to 25. He retired from the FBI in 1969—"It's a young man's job"—and spent another 14 years in the area with Martin Marietta Aerospace.

He still shakes his head in wonder about the law breakers he encountered: a man stopped for stealing a car who volunteered that he also had killed a woman in Oregon; a con artist who kept a black book detailing the dates of his crimes, the names of victims and the amount of money taken; the husband who murdered his wife and kept the body for days in the closet of his hotel room.

At Vandenberg, a worker at the base exchange was arrested for stealing goods. Conviction was easy. "He had kept a record of everything he had taken," Nolan recalled, "including the retail price and the price that was being charged at the BX (base exchange).

"The criminal mind works in strange ways."

*By Bob Nelson, January 1987*

*Nolan's stay on the Central Coast, originally planned for one year, stretched to 25*

# A Hot Time at the Fire Station

BACK IN THE days when cities schemed and connived to get national publicity in the prestigious picture pages of *Life* magazine, Santa Maria achieved the distinction in a unique and embarrassing way:

In 1956, a firefighter's mishap set fire to the city's fire station, and all three of the municipal fire trucks went up in flames.

Mortifying, that is what it was—especially since the fire engines were not insured.

*Life* published a picture of the burned-out station and the lineup of flame-blackened vehicles with the headline "Fiery Finish for Firemen's Fire Engines."

To some Santa Marians the fire was a joke. Who ever heard of a fire department burning its own engines, neatly lined up inside their station? But city officials, who were out of town when the fire erupted, did not see the joke—only the cost and the civic discomfiture.

The fire happened because the lone firefighter on duty mistook gasoline for water—and then turned a small blaze into a disaster by dropping an open five-gallon can of gasoline on the flames.

The Santa Maria fire station in 1956 was a one-story, tile-roofed extension of the present city hall, stretching eastward along Cook Street, where the parking lot for city hall is today. It had been built in 1937 for $17,000.

The fire department force consisted of three paid firefighters plus volunteers who rushed to the station whenever the siren wailed.

On the morning of Friday, May 25, one of the three firefighters, Raymond Smith, was drinking coffee alone in the firehouse kitchen when he noticed a small puddle under the city's best engine, No. 6.

"I thought it was water because No. 6 had a leaky drain valve and had leaked on previous occasions," he stated in his official report. "Getting up from the table, I walked around to No. 6, opened the valve, and slammed it shut in an effort to stop the leakage ..."

After coffee, Smith decided to gas up the fire trucks; that is, top off their tanks with fuel so they would have full tanks when they rolled on the next alarm. He brought a five-gallon can of gasoline from the storeroom, removed the stopper from the top, and started down between the No. 6 and No. 3 engines. As he did so, he noticed that the puddle had grown larger.

"I reached for a mop to mop it up and swoosh, it ignited," he told a *Santa Maria Times* reporter the day of the fire.

Several days later, in his official report, Smith described the scene in slightly different terms: "What had previously appeared to be a pool of water under Engine No. 6 suddenly mushroomed into a wall of flame.

"It was such a surprising and unexpected development I dropped the can of gasoline I was carrying ..."

Just how the firefighter handled both the mop and the can of gasoline is uncertain. So is the way in which the puddle of gasoline actually ignited. Nobody else was in the building to give an account.

The flames burned his trousers and his left hand. He ran to a faucet at the rear of the engine room and doused water on himself. Next, with the flames spreading, Smith tried to sound the fire siren that would summon the volunteer firefighters. But the siren had shorted out and would not emit a note.

The firefighter then ran to the city administrator's office in the main building to call the police. They called the water department, which turned on an old World War II air raid alarm.

Its screech alerted the townspeople. A man leaving city hall saw flames flashing out beneath the doors of the fire station. A school crossing guard rushed into the police station to report seeing smoke and flame.

Volunteers hurried to the fire station by car and on foot, ready to attack the blazing building with fire hoses. But no fire hoses were to be had; all were inside the building and could not be reached. One brave soul climbed on the roof of city hall with a garden hose and tried to keep the fire from spreading into the main building. Smith wanted to help but was taken to a doctor for treatment.

Meanwhile, calls for help had been made to surrounding communities. Fire trucks rolled from Guadalupe, Lompoc, Orcutt, Nipomo and the county station at the Santa Maria airport.

With their hoses, much larger water streams were turned on the fire, but by then it was too late.

Smoke spread through the main portion of city hall, and evacuation of the building was ordered. Employees and volunteers began hauling records and office furniture to safety. Dozens of people pitched in to help. One, Mildred Ferguson, arrived with coffee and cookies for the firefighters.

One photograph in the *Times* showed a man neatly dressed in a dark business suit, torn between doing his civic duty and worrying about getting his clothing soiled, warily putting a hand on a fire hose as though it were a slimy snake.

For Mayor Curtis Tunnell, who had been in office only a few days, the fire was a distressing experience. He was in Monterey attending a League of California Cities convention along with three other councilmen, the city administrator and various other municipal officials. The fourth councilman was on grand jury duty in Santa Barbara.

Where was Fire Chief Frank W. Crakes? In Santa Barbara, studying how to fight fires.

Reminiscing recently about the episode, Tunnell recalled how he received the word. "They flashed a message on the screen of the Monterey theater where we were meeting, telling me to go out to the office for a phone call.

"We all got in our cars and started for Santa Maria."

*Where was Fire Chief Frank W. Crakes? In Santa Barbara, studying how to fight fires*

**The Santa Maria fire station and its three uninsured fire trucks were a total loss after a 1956 fire, as the world learned in this *Life* magazine photograph.**

Tunnell realized that no major city official was on the scene to take charge, so before leaving Monterey, he telephoned Leonard Peterson, whom he had just succeeded as mayor, and asked that he go to the station and organize things.

As the fire burned itself out, the smoking wreckage of the fire engines was pulled onto the driveway. Smith's automobile and a motorcycle belonging to firefighter Wright Crakes were also destroyed.

With its fire department ruined, Santa Maria faced the prospect of no fire protection. Help from other government agencies, however, prevented such a dangerous situation. A Lompoc fire truck and two county trucks stayed at the scene until two county Civil Defense engines arrived from Santa Barbara. Placed on indefinite loan to the city, they were stationed on the street to answer alarms.

Ultimately, a new station was constructed across the street at the southeast corner of Cook and McClelland streets.

After the embers and emotions cooled, city officials determined that a capital outlay of about $50,000 would be needed to replace the fire trucks and equipment.

While community gossip made much of the fact that the fire engines had not been insured, the lack of insurance was actually a planned gamble. Only the vehicles themselves were uninsured; all ladders and other equipment on them were covered. So was the building.

The mayor explained in a statement to the community: "If we had had insurance on the fire trucks, we could have collected an amount not exceeding $10,000. If this amount were to be balanced against the amount of premiums which the city would have paid all these years, you can easily see the city had saved money by carrying its own fire and collision insurance."

After all, what were the odds against fire trucks being destroyed by fire in their own station?

*By Phillip H. Ault, October 1990*

CAR SHOPPERS AT Beattie Motors in Lompoc late in the afternoon of December 16, 1958 were shocked out of sales pitches about the new Ford Edsel Rangers by a thunderous roar coming from the bustling military base to the north.

In Orcutt, a few seconds later, the noise frightened potential new home buyers flocking to see the $17,500 models at Oak Knoll Estates. They looked up to see a white contrail arching thousands of feet into the sky.

All over the Central Coast, people suddenly remembered that the Air Force had made announcements about "some launch," but none of them knew what to expect.

What they had witnessed was the free world's first firing of a ballistic missile under push-button warfare circumstances—an opening round in what became "The Space Race" with the Soviet Union. The flight put newly commissioned Vandenberg Air Force Base into headlines around the world, with economic vibrations on the Central Coast that are felt to this day.

Missile contrails have etched the skies almost 1700 times in the past 35 years. Most have been highly successful; some—especially in recent years—have been embarrassing failures. But none was more significant than the first Thor missile launch that covered 1500 miles in about 15 minutes.

At the time, the "missile gap" was on everyone's mind. America had not yet developed an intercontinental ballistic missile capability. Our chief adversary, the Soviet Union, was way ahead.

The Soviets had announced on August 27, 1957 that they had successfully flight-tested "a super long-distance intercontinental multi-stage ballistic missile" that had flown "at a very high, unprecedented altitude." This feat, they announced, would "make it possible to reach remote areas without resorting to a strategic air force."

Then, on October 4, 1957, they launched Sputnik—the world's first artificial satellite. On November 3 came Sputnik II; its passenger, a dog named Lakia, surveyed the heavens and the earth from inside its 1120-pound satellite. A sense of panic led to major changes in the American missile and space program.

One of the key requirements for the Air Force was to find a base where missiles, combat crews and their supporting ground equipment could be tested under realistic conditions. Since facilities at Cape Canaveral, FL were not designed to support such activities, the Air Force canvassed nearly 200 government-owned tracts of land in search of the site of America's first combat-ready missile base.

Camp Cooke near Lompoc then was merely another inactive army post. Closed at the end of World War II, it had reopened during the Korean War only to again be shut down. Sheep grazed among its 2000 slowly deteriorating wooden buildings.

Despite its shabby appearance, Camp Cooke stood out

# FIRST FLIGHT: THE MISSILE ERA AT VANDENBERG

The massive Thor missile travels through Lompoc on its way to the bustling new Vandenberg Air Force Base.

from other sites for several reasons. Since it was large and remote, it could easily accommodate many missile launchers that could be built at safe distances from civilian communities and the base's living areas.

Most important, missiles could be launched to the west or south over the ocean without presenting a danger to inhabited areas.

In June 1956 a site selection board recommended that all of Camp Cooke lying north of the Santa Ynez River—some 64,000 acres—should become Cooke Air Force Base. The land south of the river was transferred to the Navy and became Point Arguello Missile Test Range. Work began in May 1957.

Within a couple of years, nearly 20,000 men and women would be busy building facilities to test missiles, launch earth satellites, train combat-ready crews for other Air Force bases, and house missiles that would stand strategic alert—ready, if need be, to return the fire of any aggressor.

In October 1958 there was a name change to Vandenberg Air Force Base to honor Gen. Hoyt S. Vandenberg, the service's second chief of staff. Two months later, after much sweat and toil, the date for the first launch arrived.

The pressure on Vandenberg to succeed was intensified when the Air Force announced it was planning to demonstrate a two-ocean launch capability by having both Vandenberg and Cape Canaveral launch Thors on the same day.

On the appointed day, the weather was sunny and warm with only a slight breeze. About 200 newsmen from around the world watched and reported from their vantage point on a mesa 8200 feet from the launch site. Even the Southern Pacific got into the act. The railroad brought in a mobile concession car to feed reporters, company officials and visiting dignitaries.

As could be expected for a first launch, there were equipment problems up and down the test range, plus three delays for passings trains. Each event caused the launch to be held. Hours slipped by, and the coastal fog began rolling in.

Then came the announcement that the launch was "T minus 15 minutes to go and counting." Anxiety mounted as the minutes passed. All eyes were sharply focused on launch pad 75-1.

Cold, inanimate, lifeless, the Thor pointed toward the heavens. "T-minus 1," shouted the announcer. The next 60 seconds were the longest anyone watching had ever lived.

At last, at 3:44:45, the "fuse was lit." Columns of vapor billowed from beneath the Thor with a tremendous roar. Flame poured out of the ground—vented through a launch duct.

Ever so slowly, the 65 foot-long missile started to move upward. Then it picked up speed as the tremendous power of the engines took hold under the tail and pushed the 100,000 pounds of dead weight. The Thor majestically rose from the pad that only 17 months before had been a sandy wasteland.

In awe, people arched their necks to look upward, straining to watch the wingless bird through the quickly setting sun. Soon all that could be seen was a pinpoint of flame.

Almost as suddenly as it had begun, the show was over. It had only been three minutes since launch, but the deadly white dart was out of sight—racing toward its target at speeds that would approach 10,000 mph. It landed five miles from its target point in the Pacific—amazing accuracy for the day.

Similar success for the Cape Canaveral launch the same day demonstrated the Air Force's two-ocean punch.

December 16, 1958 would always be remembered as a special day at the base. There could never be another "first flight from Vandenberg" and the dawn of a new and exciting era for the Central Coast.

*By Cary Gray, December 1993*

**A few years later the base was the site of a simultaneous launching of two Minuteman missiles.**

*Photos/Vandenberg Air Force Base and Lompoc Valley Historical Society*

A Santa Maria barbecue crew in 1904. Half a century later, local barbecuers would discover tri-tip.

*Photo/Santa Maria Valley Historical Society*

# THE LEGEND OF TRI-TIP

T RI-TIP IS NO *longer our little gastronomical secret. It is found on more and more meat counters in Southern California and Bay Area markets as city dwellers begin to discover a taste that folks on the Central Coast have enjoyed for decades.*

*But the triangular cut of beef still is greeted by a "What's that?" from visitors and newcomers when it appears on local menus and barbecue pits.*

Central Coast *magazine answered the question by providing the lore of tri-tip as well as its traditional method of preparation. The result is an expanding league of tri-tip aficionados which may someday spread the word to woefully uninformed meat-eaters in Dallas, Chicago, maybe even New York City.*

First, some background. Butchers refer to tri-tip as "bottom sirloin," part of the top sirloin and part of the sirloin tip, said Mike Dykes, owner of Arroyo Grande Meat Co., a custom meat market.

"In the old days," he explained, "the butchers had a cut they called the 'standard cut' which had top sirloin on one side, the bone in the middle, then the filet, and the tail part was the tri-tip. Only nobody knew it."

Somebody who did know it was a Texas meat man whom Dykes remembered as "Mr. Tri-tip."

"He brought all this tri-tip to California, tons of it" said Dykes, a butcher for 30 years. "But he couldn't sell it, so it was used for ground beef."

The breakthrough, according to local barbecuers, came in the late 1950s when Santa Maria butcher Bob Schoups innocently placed the end cut—seasoned with salt, pepper and garlic salt—on a rack in his department's rotisserie. Forty-five minutes later he shared it with fellow workers who were amazed at its unique texture and flavor.

Schoups promoted his tri-tip and taught customers how to prepare it. Williams Brothers (later Vons markets) picked up the idea and began to market tri-tip through its Central Coast chain where customers quickly came to appreciate its taste and—at least at that time—low price compared to other cuts of beef.

Preparation is the key. In the hands of an unprepared cook, tri-tip can become a very tough piece of meat.

The basic recipe for success remains the same: oakwood logs are placed in a pit with movable grate and burned until red-hot. Backyard chefs also can use charcoal mixed with oakwood chips and bark available at local markets. Once lit, the fire should be hot but not blazing. A Los Alamos beef expert advised, "Put your hand over the screen, and if you can count to 10, then the fire is ready. If you can count only to three or four before removing your hand, then the fire is too hot."

Veteran barbecuer Larry Viegas offered these tips:

• Do not trim off the fat before putting the meat on the grill. By placing the fat side over the fire first, the juice will come up through the meat and make it tender.

• Sear the lean part of the meat over the fire for 5 to 10 minutes to seal in the juices, then flip over to the fat side for 30 to 45 minutes, depending on the size of the cut and the desired degree of doneness. When juice appears at the top of the meat, it is time to flip for another 30-45 minutes.

• The fat can easily be trimmed after cooking.

Although traditionalists season their tri-tip with salt, pepper and garlic salt, the cut "is so versatile you can make it taste any way you want," said Dykes.

*By Bob Nelson, July 1991*